Life's Greatest
Quest

to become more like Christ

Clark Logan

JOHN RITCHIE LTD
CHRISTIAN PUBLICATIONS

40 Beansburn, Kilmarnock, Scotland

ISBN-13: 978 1 904064 95 4
ISBN-10: 1 904064 95 7

Copyright © 2010 by John Ritchie Ltd.
40 Beansburn, Kilmarnock, Scotland

www.ritchiechristianmedia.co.uk

Typeset by John Ritchie Ltd., Kilmarnock
Printed by Bell & Bain Ltd., Glasgow

LIFE'S GREATEST QUEST
to become more like Christ

*In thankfulness to God
for my parents*

Contents

Foreword

It is with pleasure I write this foreword as I have known the writer since he was a small boy attending the meetings of the local assembly of Christians in Dundonald. Since his conversion he has shown a deep and real interest in the things of God. His manner and attitude have earned him the love, respect and interest of the entire assembly.

When he was exercised about the work of the Lord in Botswana, our brethren were united and wholehearted in the commendation of Clark and his wife. Indeed, some of the overseers have gone to see and rejoice with him in the progress of the work. Missionaries in many lands are burdened about the need of younger men and women to answer the call of God and give help in these needy lands.

I have read with interest and profit something of the teaching of this book and while it shows afresh the writer's devotion, it will also be challenging, inspiring and instructive. I trust it will be used of God in the exaltation of Christ and the blessing of His people.

James G. Hutchinson
Newtownards
N Ireland
Sept 2009

The Challenge

"Is Jesus Christ like you?"

—An African chief

The question startled him! It was so unexpected, and unnerving. The missionary had been witnessing to the chief concerning the Lord Jesus Christ. Sitting under a tree, over an open Bible, he had patiently explained the wonderful character of the Saviour's life. The wise old man listened carefully, and then he said, "Is Jesus Christ like you?" Here was the crux of the whole matter. It was a relatively simple thing to speak of Christ, but it was a far greater challenge to display Christ in one's life.

If others form their view of Christ from the example of our lives, then what sort of impression do we make? If we are not like Him, we will misrepresent Him, no matter how eloquent our words of testimony might be. More than anything else, this troubled world needs to see Christ in us who have believed in Him.

Introduction

The world today is preoccupied with outward accomplishment. People who get things done are admired and emulated as role models. A project completed, a plan fulfilled or a target attained are regarded as the true measures of success. In support of this viewpoint we are often told that the private life of a person is his or her own business and has no significant bearing on public life and fitness to do the job. In other words, character is not important; what matters are results.

Most Christians would not agree with this assessment, and yet many of us still feel drawn to praise the outward appearances of success, even in Christian life and service. So it is that gospel preachers who report numerous conversions, Bible teachers who draw large audiences or missionaries who have planted many churches can all be set on a pedestal. But God will ever go beneath the surface to the heart of a man. He alone is able to do this.

The underlying theme of this book is that God is as interested in what we are *becoming* as in what we are *doing*. His work in us is as important as His work through us. These two aspects of life are not mutually exclusive – what we are inevitably affects what we do – but we all tend to excuse or disguise lack of inner spiritual development by pointing to the outer accomplishments.

The first section of the book sets the scene by focusing on God's great delight in Christ. Against this background, the Scriptural basis for our main conviction is laid – God's chief desire and purpose for us is that we should become more like His Son.

The second section emphasizes the inner life of Christ. Success in secret always precedes power in public: Christ is our great example in this. Our own personal relationship with God, our submission to His Spirit and our obedience to His Word are all vital in the development of true Christian character. God starts His work from within and the greatest battles of life are fought and won in the inner man.

Starting with the second section, each chapter (3-17) ends with a *Personal Reminder*: a short pointed challenge summarizing a number of key points. These are not at all comprehensive nor should they be considered as a mandatory checklist; their purpose is to encourage us to apply the truth of each chapter in a practical way.

The middle section focuses on the public ministry of Christ: what He said and what He did. Personal relationships lay at the heart of His ministry and we will see His deep love for others. He treated individuals as those created in God's image, even when the image was so marred by sin as to be almost unrecognizable. The closing events of Christ's life upon earth – His death and burial, resurrection and ascension – have implications for us as believers in our close association with Him.

In the fourth section, we consider the present ministry of Christ for us in heaven. He is supporting us every step of the way as we travel through life. When we consider His offices as our Great High Priest, our Shepherd, Advocate and Friend, we gain insights into the care that He has for His own. He would expect us to share that same care for others.

In the fifth and final section, we look forward to the future. The One who has *lifted us up* out of our sins and who now is *bearing us up* on the journey home, will one day *take us up* and take us in to heaven itself to be with Him. There His glory will be manifested and we will share in it with Him; indeed, we will reign with Him. Best of all, we shall be like Him for ever!

But for today, each one of us can strive for this supreme goal of becoming more like Christ now. It would be a tragedy if we were to neglect life's greatest quest and arrive safely in heaven, but miss His commendation and forfeit our eternal reward.

There are many Christians whose lives are largely unnoticed, except by the eye of God. And yet they have allowed the Spirit of God to refine their natures, and through their warm devotion and faithfulness to Christ, "the beauty of Jesus" is seen in them. One day these shall have their reward and hear Him say, "Well done!" Yes, heaven will be full of surprises.

I wish to thank the directors and staff of John Ritchie Ltd, and the editors of the *Believer's Magazine* who have encouraged me over the years. Special thanks are due to my friend, Dr Bert Cargill: since I wrote to him some months ago, enclosing a tentative outline for this book and a summary of the ideas that have been turning over in my mind and heart for many years, he has given generously of his time, editorial skills and counsel at every stage. I also thank Dr Andrew Logan who read the complete draft and made valuable suggestions during evening discussions with his father, until long after midnight. A warm note of appreciation and thanks is due to Mr James G. Hutchinson; with over sixty years of experience in the Lord's service, he graciously agreed to write the Foreword. As we say in Botswana when we are profoundly grateful, *Ke lebogile go menaganye!*

Clark Logan
Tlokweng
Botswana
Sept 2009

CHAPTER 1

God's Pleasure in Christ –
A Unique Person

No one has ever pleased God as Christ did. When He left heaven and came down to earth, He was acting in perfect obedience to His Father. In taking upon Himself human form, His divine character did not change; perfect humanity was added to deity. Although the mystery of His incarnation is beyond our full understanding, we can appreciate in a measure the beauties and moral glories of His unique person. As we search the Scriptures and learn of Him, we are challenged to become more like Him.

His Divine Approval

God expressed His delight in Christ at His baptism. Mark, the Gospel writer, tells us that the heavens were rent asunder and a voice declared, "Thou art my beloved Son, in whom I am well pleased" (Mk 1.11). This approval from the Father spanned those years spent quietly in Nazareth. At every moment and in every detail of His life He pleased the Father.

Later, on a mountaintop in Galilee, the same voice was heard from a cloud saying, "This is my beloved Son: hear him" (Mk 9.7). On that occasion three disciples were granted a wonderful preview of His coming glory. Looking back or looking forward, God's commendation was the same.

God's manifest pleasure in Christ did not just begin when the

Lord Jesus came to earth. The eternal Son and the Father were in close communion long before the worlds were made: "I was set up from everlasting, from the beginning, or ever the earth was…Then I was by him, as one brought up with him: and I was daily his delight, rejoicing always before him" (Pro 8.23, 30).

Other prophetic Scriptures, written long before Christ came, tell of the Father's thoughts concerning His Son. In Isaiah, we read of God's pleasure in Him: "Behold, my servant, whom I uphold; mine elect, in whom my soul delighteth; I have put my spirit upon him." We read also of His meekness: "He shall not cry, nor lift up, nor cause his voice to be heard in the street. A bruised reed shall he not break, and the smoking flax shall he not quench" (Isa 42.1-3). Another reference tells of His sufferings: "Behold, my servant shall deal prudently, he shall be exalted and extolled, and be very high. As many were astonied at thee; his visage was so marred more than any man, and his form more than the sons of men…For he shall grow up before him as a tender plant, and as a root out of a dry ground …He is brought as a lamb to the slaughter, and as a sheep before her shearers is dumb, so he openeth not his mouth" (Isa 52.13; 53.2, 7). When it came to describing His sufferings, there was nothing with which they could be compared. They were *more than* anything known to men. What a price was paid for our redemption!

Christ's desire to please the Father was the reason He left His home in heaven and came down to earth. Although He was the eternal Son of God, He "took upon him the form of a servant and was made in the likeness of men" (Phil 2.7). The perfect Servant expressed the desires of His heart in this way: "My meat is to do the will of him that sent me, and to finish his work"; "I do always those things that please him" (Jn 4.34; 8.29). In the agony of Gethsemane, before moving forward to the cross, the words of His anguished prayer summed up the whole of His life: "Not my will, but thine, be done" (Lk 22.42). The essence of sin is self-will and independence from God. The obedient and dependent Son of God was sinless through and through: this fitted Him to go to Calvary as the only perfect sacrifice for a world of sinners.

Following His shameful death upon the cross and His triumphant resurrection, God has "highly exalted him, and given him a name which is above every name" (Phil 2.9). Christ now occupies the place of honour and authority at God's right hand, but there is a day yet to come when there will be universal acknowledgment of His worth. Every knee will bow and every tongue will confess that He is Lord, to the glory of God the Father (Phil 2.10).

His Physical Features

Strange as it may seem, we know almost nothing about the physical appearance of the Lord Jesus Christ, except that His body was scarred from the experiences of Calvary. In those last few hours before His death upon the cross, many kinds of wounds were inflicted upon Him: He sustained abrasions and bruises, lacerations and penetrating injuries, as His enemies heaped their scorn and hatred upon Him.

One kind of wound described in forensic medicine was conspicuously absent – the defence wound. Such wounds are commonly found on the body of one who has resisted attack. The backs of the forearms are bruised and lacerated as the victim has sought instinctively to ward off the blows and shield his face in self-defence. The Lord Jesus had none of these. He offered no resistance whatsoever when He was led as a lamb to the slaughter.

In heaven today there is only one man in bodily form, our blessed Saviour, and the marks of Calvary are plain for all to see; these will be an eternal reminder of His love for us. We who know Him have a sure and certain hope of seeing Him, and we shall instantly recognize Him. Even Israel, who rejected

Him, in a coming day will look upon the One they pierced. Sadder still, every eye will see Him "and all the kindreds of the earth shall wail because of Him" (Rev 1.7). Their sorrow and tears will be a prelude to their eternal judgment.

Perhaps one of the reasons why the Scriptures are silent about the physical appearance of the Lord Jesus Christ is that, by the standards of heaven, this matter is not important. The spiritual takes precedence over the physical; it is the moral beauty of Christ that God desires to see in us. None of us should feel disadvantaged by any physical weakness or limitation we might have; each of us can make progress in seeking to be more like Him.

At the same time, we should understand that Christ has many other divine glories that are exclusively His and that set Him uniquely above all others. Let us mention just a few of these:

His Divine Glories
1. Unique Knowledge
Christ is omniscient; He has perfect knowledge. When He was here upon earth He displayed a unique self-awareness as to His true identity and His reason for being here; He also revealed an intimate knowledge of the minds and hearts of others.

As He grew up in Nazareth, His physical and mental growth was appropriate for every stage of His human development. Luke tells us that "the child grew, and waxed strong in spirit, filled with wisdom: and the grace of God was upon him" (Lk 2.40), and later, "Jesus increased in wisdom and stature, and in favour with God and man" (Lk 2.52). But there was something else that set Him apart: He knew that He had come to earth to walk a path of suffering that would lead to His death upon the cross. On one occasion, when He was just a boy, He asked His mother, "wist ye not that I must be about my Father's business?" (Lk 2.49). His words did not refer to Joseph (His boyhood guardian), but to God and the work the Father had given His

Son to do. The day came when He stood up in the synagogue in Nazareth and read from Isaiah 61 concerning the ministry of the promised Messiah. As the people watched Him, He declared, "This day is this scripture fulfilled in your ears" (Lk 4.21).

On three occasions He predicted His own violent death and triumphant resurrection. The writer, John, tells us repeatedly that Christ knew that the Scriptures must be fulfilled (Jn 13.18; 15.25; 17.12; 18.9; 19.28); He had a specific and detailed knowledge of what He referred to as His "hour". That period included His betrayal and mock trial, the suffering inflicted by men, and the terrible judgment poured upon Him by God when He hung upon the cross.

At first, John recorded that Christ knew His hour had not yet come (Jn 2.4; 7.30; 8.20). Attempts by others to accelerate His death were all in vain. From John chapter 12 onwards, however, there is a significant change: in the week preceding His crucifixion He declared, "The hour is come, that the Son of Man should be glorified. Verily, verily, I say unto you, Except a corn of wheat fall into the ground and die, it abideth alone: but if it die, it bringeth forth much fruit … Now is my soul troubled; and what shall I say? Father, save me from this hour: but for this cause came I unto this hour. Father, glorify thy name" (Jn 12.23-28). In chapter 13, He was with the disciples in the upper room in Jerusalem just before the Passover feast. We are told, "Jesus knew that his hour was come that he should depart out of this world unto the Father" (Jn 13.1). Later, He addressed God in prayer and said, "Father, the hour is come" (Jn 17.1). He was aware that the flow of events was leading to a climax; He knew of "all things that should come upon him" (Jn 18.4). And finally, at the end of the three hours of darkness upon the cross, He knew that the work of salvation was complete (Jn 19.28).

Apart from the Lord's knowledge of Himself and His calling, He displayed a unique and perfect knowledge of others. Again, if we confine ourselves to John's Gospel, we discover two remarkable statements: "He knew all men" and "He knew what was in man" (Jn 2.24-25). He knew what was particular and individual to each man, as well as that which was common to all men.

Consider His words to Nathaniel – it is likely that they had never met before – when Christ spoke of Nathaniel's honest character. When he questioned how the Lord could possibly know him, Christ replied, "Before that Philip called thee, when thou wast under the fig tree, I saw thee" (Jn 1.48). He was the One who knew the hearts of men: His eye saw the unseen; His ear heard the unspoken. He knew the thoughts and motives of those who questioned His words or opposed His teaching. He even knew the identity of His betrayer (6.61, 64; 13.11).

2. Unique Power

Another divine attribute displayed by Christ was omnipotence. He had power over nature, power over illness and power over death. Of the nine miracles that displayed His power over nature, five had to do with the sea and four with the land. He dealt with a storm on Galilee by commanding the wind and the waves to be still; there was an instantaneous calm. During another storm, He walked on the water to reach the fearful band of disciples in the boat. On two occasions He directed the disciples as they fished so that large catches were recorded. He assisted Peter to find tribute money in the mouth of a fish. Twice He fed thousands of people with just a few loaves and fishes. He changed water into wine, and not by any sleight of hand. There was only one miracle linked with judgment and that was the cursing of the fig tree.

There were twenty-three separate miracles of healing in which He met a great variety of need amongst those who were sick and suffering. At other times a whole community was healed (Mk 1.33-34). He could draw near and bring relief with a touch; He could also remain at a distance and cure with a word. The last miracle of healing took place when His enemies came to arrest Him. Peter rashly drew his sword and cut off a man's ear; the Lord responded by healing him instantly. The Great Physician never lost a case.

It is recorded that He raised three individuals from the dead: Jairus's daughter had just died; the widow of Nain's son was being carried to his burial; and Lazarus had been dead in the tomb for four days so that the body had begun to decompose. Truly, Christ is not only the creator but also the restorer of all physical and spiritual life. It is no wonder that they said of Him, "He hath done all things well" (Mk 7.37).

3. Unique Holiness
The holiness of Christ exceeds that of any other person; however, the Scriptures go further and teach that He alone was absolutely holy and not the faintest trace of sin was found in Him. His thought life was pure and untainted; His words were ever true; His actions always glorified His Father, God. This sets Him apart from all others.

The holiness of the Son of God is linked to His deity; the two cannot be separated. When Christ was made flesh, absolute deity was combined with perfect humanity. The first was not diminished to make way for the second. His humanity was not like that of Adam's in being innocent; His was unique in being perfect and morally in harmony with His deity. He could not sin because He was God manifest in flesh (1 Tim 3.16).

Just before His birth, the angel announced His coming to Mary in this way: "that holy thing that shall be born of thee shall be called the Son of God" (Lk 1.35). Christ spoke of the devil coming to tempt Him, but finding nothing in Him that would respond to any enticement to sin (Jn 14.30). Pilate found no fault in Him after his wife had acknowledged that Jesus was a just man. Even the false witnesses could not agree on anything that would have compromised His innocence. The centurion was amazed at the spectacle before Him and exclaimed, "Truly this was the Son of God" (Mt 27.54).

Later, three New Testament writers restated these truths in their own particular way. These references are much loved and frequently quoted: Peter tells us that He did no sin (1 Pet 2.22); Paul says that He knew no sin (2 Cor 5.21); and John declares that in Him is no sin (1 Jn 3.5). Not a thought was ever out of place; not a word ever needed to be retracted; not a step ever had to be retraced. With total confidence we can trust the Word of God that proclaims both the deity and humanity of the incarnate Son of God.

His Moral Beauties

Christ stands supreme: His divine glory and power are uniquely His alone. We will never be able to attain to any such perfection here upon earth; but we can and should aspire to a deeper knowledge of His Word, a greater measure of power in service and an increasing holiness in our own lives. We can become more like Him day by day and reflect something of His moral beauties and excellence.

Where might we start? Take any cluster of glories you can find in the Scriptures and He embodies them all. We see His surpassing excellence in every aspect and in every combination. He has no strong points because He has no weak points. He radiates true beauty as a sparkling, flawless, perfectly cut diamond.

Paul wrote to the Galatians of the fruit of the Spirit as being "love, joy, peace, longsuffering, gentleness, goodness, faith, meekness, temperance" (Gal 5.22-23). All of this fruit was constantly displayed in the life of Christ. The same apostle exhorted the Ephesians to "take unto you the whole armour of God" which included truth, righteousness and faith (Eph 6.13-18). Christ was never less than fully armed and always vigilant in the constant battle against the enemy. Paul also urged the Colossians to "Put on therefore, as the elect of God, holy and beloved, bowels of mercies, kindness, humbleness of mind, meekness, longsuffering … And above all these things put on charity, which is the bond of perfectness" (Col 3.12-14). All of these garments were Christ's daily apparel and love covered them all.

He was full of grace and truth, love and mercy, strength and boldness, gentleness and meekness, purity and holiness, humility and selflessness, joy and pleasantness, truth and righteousness, patience and endurance, kindness and generosity. These are just a select number of the moral beauties found in Christ.

Anyone who has ever attempted to describe Him has ended up feeling completely inadequate for the task. We must confess that our minds are too small and our words are too feeble. Perhaps the best we can do is to echo the words of another – "He is altogether lovely" (Song 5.16).

CHAPTER 2

God's Purpose For Us –
To Be Like Christ

God is a God of grace who reveals Himself to men and in His Word we read of His great eternal purposes for us. He wants us to know what He has done for us in the past, what He expects from us now, and what He has in store for us in the future. He desires to fit us for heavenly citizenship by us becoming more like Christ today. We need be in no doubt as to what Christ is like for He came down to earth and lived amongst men. And we have a divinely inspired record of those who witnessed His pathway upon earth and testified to what He said and did.

Let us now examine a number of key Scripture verses that deal with our main theme:

The Divine Purpose
"For whom he did foreknow, he also did predestinate to be conformed to the image of his Son, that he might be the firstborn among many brethren" (Rom 8.29).
God wants to change us. When we trusted in Christ for salvation, we changed direction; we had been travelling to eternal judgment but we turned round to start journeying to eternal joy. Before conversion, each day saw us drawing nearer to hell but then, having been born again, we began to head for heaven. That sudden reversal was neither the whole story nor the end of the matter, but just the beginning. Although every one of us needs to change and keep on changing, we are

frequently resistant to it. The truth is this – if we are to become what we should be, we must be prepared to leave behind what we presently are.

If we are self-satisfied and content with ourselves at present, it is unlikely that we will see any need for change. If, on the other hand, we are brave enough to make a true assessment of ourselves and humble enough to accept it, then God can enable us to be strong enough to do something about it, and change for the better. It would be sad if, for example, those who were known to be short-tempered in their pre-conversion days remained short-tempered as believers and went home to heaven just the same. Salvation always changes a person but that change must continue. Sometimes we stall.

In his letter to the Romans, Paul explains the truth of the gospel: the need of salvation (ch 1-3); the means of it (ch 4); the results of it (ch 5-8); the scope of it (ch 9-11); and the responsibilities of it (ch 12-16). Basically, he is saying that we are sinners who need to be saved; then, following salvation, we must continue to be sanctified and live as saints in the world.

In chapter 8 there are frequent references to the presence and power of the Holy Spirit in God's children. His work in us has a great divine purpose and, whatever our understanding of divine foreknowledge and predestination might be, what is clear is that God's plan for all of us who belong to Him is that we should be conformed to the image of His Son.

The Human Response

"That I may know him, and the power of his resurrection, and the fellowship of his sufferings, being made conformable unto his death" (Phil 3.10).

Paul sought to fulfil all the purposes of God for his life. He wanted to lay hold of those things for which God had laid hold of him. His life demonstrated the true and wholehearted nature of his response to the divine claims upon him.

The whole tenor of this verse is that of a burning desire to advance and to change. It was more than just wishful thinking on Paul's part; he applied himself with unswerving devotion to realizing his goal. He was never satisfied with his life in the sense of feeling that he had arrived at the state which God desired for him; there were things he had yet to attain. He kept stretching forward and climbing higher in his spiritual experience.

It is true that he already knew Christ as his Saviour and Lord, but he sought to know Him better. The centre and circumference of his life was not a creed but a Person. It was his avowed aim "to win Christ, and be found in him" (Phil 3.8-9). In truth he could say, "For to me to live is Christ" (Phil 1.21). Even in death he wanted to be able to magnify his Lord. Christ was everything to Paul and he was prepared to face any circumstance, so long as he could know more of His Lord. He regarded all earthly advantages as only refuse; indeed, he had discarded them for something better – the surpassing excellence of getting to know Christ.

The power he had already experienced in his ministry, he desired to know in greater measure. Paul first encountered the risen Christ on the Damascus road. That day he realized that the man, Jesus, whose followers he had so vehemently opposed, was none other than the Lord! The crucified One was now the risen and glorified One. Christ had all authority to command His followers to carry on His work, and He had all the power through His Spirit to enable them to obey.

Paul willingly endured many severe trials because of his allegiance to Christ (2 Cor 11.23-28). In his mind and heart he was able to identify even more closely with the Lord when those sufferings came. It was as if he was bound together with Christ in them; there was a fellowship in them and a sharing of them. He would have been the first to admit that as a sinner himself, he could never have had any part in the atoning sufferings of

Christ upon the cross for man's sin; nevertheless, he was willing to face the inevitable persecution that those who are faithful to Christ are called upon to endure in a hostile world.

He was prepared to be like his Lord even to the extent of being ready to sacrifice his own life for the sake of others. He also desired to be identified more and more with all that the cross declared. It told out man's hatred and rejection of all that was of God; Paul was fully prepared to suffer reproach at the hands of men. It declared God's holy opposition to sin; Paul sought to live a life in which sin was judged and forsaken. The cross also told out the matchless love of God for sinners, and Paul lived his life to tell out that love to others. Day by day he sought to experience an ongoing change to become more like his Lord. His life of total commitment to Christ stands as a great inspiration to us all.

The Present Process
"But we all, with open face beholding as in a glass the glory of the Lord, are changed into the same image from glory to glory, even as by the Spirit of the Lord" (2 Cor 3.18).
As we focus daily upon Christ and see more of His beauties, those same beauties will be reflected in our own lives. This will happen gradually (even unconsciously, at times) and be a lifetime process. There will be growth, an increase in likeness to Christ, and a wonderful transformation. By the power of the indwelling Spirit we will be changed and Christ's glory will be seen in us too.

Under grace, every believer has access into the immediate presence of the Lord. Initially, under law, it was Moses alone who had that privilege of ascending the mountain to meet with God; however, when he left the presence of God and came down from the mountain, the reflected glory that shone from his face soon faded (2 Cor 3.13). How different for us today! The One we gaze upon is always there for us and we have unrestricted access into His presence. We can gaze upon

Him every day and many times in the day. The more we avail ourselves of this privilege, the more we will become like Him. Daily and intimate communion with Christ will always leave its mark.

In the sporting world, top athletes are instructed in the art of visualizing. They train themselves to focus beforehand on the challenge ahead. They are taught to see themselves running their best race, breasting the tape, breaking the record and ascending the winner's podium. Their prize is only a moment of fame and a fading earthly reward.

We do not need to borrow some psychological technique to make progress in becoming more like Christ but we do need to focus, not upon an earthly prize, but upon Him, the One we know and love. Others will notice the difference and hopefully conclude that we have "been with Jesus" (Acts 4.13).

The believer who gazes upon Christ will grow and become more mature in Him. There will be a growing in *faith*; Paul said of the Thessalonians that their faith grew exceedingly (2 Thes 1.3). We will learn to become more dependent upon God and His power and less reliant upon ourselves and our own abilities. We will lean more upon His promises, even when the way is hard and the path ahead seems uncertain. We will step out into the darkness and find the rock beneath.

There ought also to be a growth in *love*, as Scripture puts it, "that your love may abound yet more and more" (Phil 1.9). This is one of the defining marks of the Christian, a love that excels mere human affection. The love which God displayed and His Son demonstrated was a costly and sacrificial love: God did not spare Him "but delivered him up for us all" (Rom 8.32); "Christ also loved the church, and gave himself for it" (Eph 5.25). True followers of Christ learn to love themselves less and to love Him more; each can say in truth, "the Son of God … loved me, and gave himself for me" (Gal 2.20). They know that they are not their own but they have been bought with a great price (1 Cor 6.19-20).

People in the western world today are obsessed with themselves – self-understanding, self-image, self-development, self-fulfilment, and a host of other related ideas pervade their minds. Popular magazines advise their readers to love themselves, respect themselves and find time for themselves. "I am the most important person in my life" would sum up the philosophy of our age.

The believer's focus is completely different. Christ is the most important one in our lives, and our love for Him should excel all other loves. And when we love Him, we will love others too. Not only will we dedicate our service to Him, but we will also seek to be a blessing to others, even when it costs us to do so. In contrast to the world's creed, our personal interests come last. John the Baptist perfectly expressed this when he confessed, "He must increase, but I must decrease" (Jn 3.30).

There should be growth in *grace* and also growth in the *knowledge* of Christ: Peter exhorted the Christians to "grow in grace, and in the knowledge of our Lord and Saviour Jesus Christ" (2 Pet 3.18). It would be wonderful to think more like the Saviour thinks and act more as He acts. Again, it is slow and painful for us to set aside our own selfish will and become moulded by His. Most of the spiritual battles that we fight are waged in the mind and heart. The giving up of self is like crucifixion, and crucifixion is acutely painful (hence the meaning of the word, 'excruciating'). Paul urged the Romans "to present your bodies a living sacrifice, holy, acceptable unto God, which is your reasonable service. And be not conformed to this world: but be ye transformed by the renewing of your mind, that ye may prove what is that good, and acceptable, and perfect will of God" (Rom 12.1-2).

The Future Reality

"Beloved, now are we the sons of God, and it doth not yet appear what we shall be: but we know that, when he shall appear, we shall be like him; for we shall see him as he is" (1 Jn 3.2).

"And as we have borne the image of the earthy, we shall also bear the image of the heavenly" (1 Cor 15.49).

These verses describe the ultimate realization of God's purposes for us when one day we will be perfectly like Christ in moral purity and beauty. After our resurrection, we will have bodies of glory and a capacity to enjoy heaven and appreciate the Saviour as we have never been able to do before. At present our vision is indistinct and our minds are limited but in that day all will be changed. God will begin revealing to us more and more of the greatness and glory of Christ.

There will be distinctions in heaven when it comes to our rewards (1 Cor 3.13-14). Someone has coined the phrase that "every cup will be full, but some will have bigger cups than others." Faithfulness down here will be rewarded up there.

The cultivation of true likeness to Christ should be our chief aim. Only with divine help can we weed out those flaws and overcome those weaknesses that make us presently so unlike our Lord. Outward success is of no account to God. What matters to Him is the measure of our conformity to His Son. This path is open to every believer, whether in a position of public prominence or not. It is a noble challenge for you and for me, requiring the very best of all that is within us. Truly, this is life's greatest quest.

CHAPTER 3

His Communion with the Father

To pray is to communicate with the living God and to enjoy fellowship with Him. Prayer is a confirmation that we believe in Him and crave His presence; we are needful of His help and thankful for His blessings. The inner man grows strong and is fortified through prayer. When we lack prayer, inevitably we lack spiritual power.

The prayer life of Christ was special. If He spent so much time in prayer, it is certain that we cannot afford to spend less. We are privileged to have different accounts of His prayers in the Gospels, including words He uttered in private. An example of this would be His anguished prayer in the Garden of Gethsemane (Mt 26.36-45): Peter, James and John had fallen asleep; there were no human witnesses of what transpired between God and His Son; and yet, we have His exact words recorded for us by the inspiration of the Spirit of God.

As we read through the Gospels, Christ is seen as the dependent Man who knew the true significance and power of prayer. We find Him praying in all sorts of places – sometimes in homes but more often outdoors on the mountainside, in the wilderness, in the Garden of Gethsemane and on the cross. He prayed in private and in public. There were regular times of prayer mingled with particular prayers in times of need. There were spontaneous expressions of thankfulness and deep mysterious groans of grief; there was joy and there was agony. Overall, we discern an atmosphere of frequent and habitual prayer that pervaded His every waking moment.

There were many specific reasons why Christ prayed; but beyond these reasons, the Father and the Son communicated with one another freely because they were bound together as one in love. We see the same within a healthy human family in which the parents and children talk together for the sheer delight of enjoying one another's company.

One prayer that never came from the lips of the Saviour was a prayer of personal confession. The sinless Saviour never needed to admit to personal failure because there was none. When He was teaching the disciples to pray, the call for forgiveness represented their needs and failings, not His.

Praying at the beginning and at the end

Luke's Gospel in particular emphasizes the prayer life of Christ. It is only he who tells us that the Lord Jesus prayed during His baptism at the beginning of His public ministry (Lk 3.21-22). Christ would have been about thirty years of age. As He was praying, "the heaven was opened, and the Holy Ghost descended in a bodily shape like a dove upon him, and a voice came from heaven, which said, Thou art my beloved Son; in thee I am well pleased."

Christ's prayer was one of dedication to the challenging work that lay ahead. Before speaking to men about God, He would speak to God about men. Though He was sinless and needed no personal repentance, He identified Himself with the message and ministry of the Messiah's forerunner, John the Baptist, in fulfilment of the Word of God. His baptism was also a moment of divine approval and anointing. How should we begin any work for God? Christ has shown us – begin with prayer.

It was the same at the end of the journey as He hung upon the cross, when at last the suffering in the darkness was over and the judgment had been fully exacted. With great dignity and strength, the Saviour bowed His head and simply committed Himself to God: "Father, into thy hands I commend my spirit" (Lk 23.46). He had finished the work the Father had given Him to do, and He ended it with a prayer.

Praying apart and praying alone

It is easy for us to become distracted when we seek to pray. Christ was often busy with crowds flocking to Him as His fame spread abroad: "The people pressed upon him to hear the word of God"; "great multitudes came together to hear, and to be healed by him of their infirmities" (Lk 5.1, 15). Following such intense activity, Christ withdrew into the wilderness to pray; He deliberately and consciously sought a quiet place where He could refresh His soul (Lk 5.16).

On another occasion He taught His disciples that when they prayed, they should retire to a room and shut the door. One reason for this was to avoid the hypocritical show of the scribes and Pharisees who loved to pray ostentatiously in public places; their sole motivation was a desire to impress others. Another good reason to withdraw was to avoid being interrupted or disturbed in this holy exercise before God.

We should have our own favourite quiet places – at home, at school or at work – where we can lift our hearts heavenward and pray. The busier we are, the more we need to maintain fellowship with God. Without such communion we can easily lose our freshness and focus in His service.

An unusual verse tells us that the Lord was alone praying and yet His disciples were with Him (Lk 9.18). How could both be true? In His personal prayer life He separated Himself from others to be alone with the Father. He never prayed with the disciples as one of them. Their needs and spiritual perceptions were very different from His.

In Luke's Gospel, the ninth chapter is seen as a turning point. After Peter's confession of Christ as the Messiah, the Lord began to speak of the pathway of suffering that would lead Him to the cross. The opposition would begin to mount as He journeyed closer to Jerusalem and Calvary, but He faced the coming events fortified by prayer.

Whilst we can find fellowship in praying with others for our common needs, there are times of crisis when we must be alone and focus only upon the Lord. He knows and understands our particular need and He will give us His undivided attention. He has passed that same way before.

Praising and Praying

Luke tells us of the miraculous provision made by the Saviour to feed a hungry multitude of well over 5,000 people (all four Gospel writers relate this incident). Christ used five barley loaves and two small fishes which had been willingly given up by one young lad. Looking not at the meagre resources or the vast crowd, but looking up to heaven, the Saviour gave thanks to God before breaking the bread and dispersing it (Lk 9.16). The outcome was that all were satisfied with what they received and twelve baskets of fragments remained. Christ's provision had more than exceeded the need.

A thankful spirit should characterize the followers of Christ; praise and prayer go together. God has promised to provide for our needs and when He does, we should give thanks to Him: this would include the regular mealtimes in the home when the family gathers around the table, as well as many other occasions in the day when we are conscious of God's abundant goodness to us and we express our appreciation to Him. Of ten lepers who were healed, it is sad to note that only one returned to give thanks to the Lord, and he was a Samaritan (Lk 17.16).

On another occasion Christ's spirit was so filled with joy that He lifted His heart to God in thanksgiving for those who believed in Him: "In that hour Jesus rejoiced in spirit, and said, I thank thee, O Father, Lord of heaven and earth, that thou hast hid these things from the wise and prudent, and hast revealed them unto babes" (Lk 10.21). This expression of praise was set against a background of rejection and unbelief in places like Chorazin, Bethsaida and Capernaum. Christ knew that His followers would be despised and belittled by others – in the eyes of the world they were infantile and foolish – but through simple faith they had become the recipients of divine truth and blessing. We too should always be quick to rejoice and give thanks when souls trust Christ. The repentance of even one soul sets the courts of heaven ringing (Lk 15.10).

As well as praising, the Lord knew what it was to intercede for others and pray for specific needs. Before He chose His first disciples, "He went out into a mountain to pray, and continued all night in prayer to God" (Lk 6.12). There was no prior consultation with anyone else other than His Father. There is no particular virtue in long prayers but it was the depth of His exercise and concern that robbed Him of sleep and kept Him on His knees, pouring out His heart to God. The vigil in the darkness yielded results in the morning. He called, chose and named twelve men whose names are now so well known to us: even the traitor, Judas, was named. What love and forbearance led the Saviour to include Judas and to treat him like the rest!

We are often in a quandary when important choices loom ahead. Sometimes panic sets in and we make the mistake of hurriedly seeking advice from many different people, long before we bring the matter to God. At other times, we have already decided what we want to do, and we bring the matter to God only for an endorsement. Perhaps we could learn from the example of the Saviour and pray *before* we make a choice.

The work of the Lord cannot be maintained without prayer. Christ chose seventy others to share in His work. After acknowledging the greatness of the harvest and the scarcity of labourers, He urged them to pray that the Lord would thrust out even more labourers into the work (Lk 10.2). The Saviour was under no illusions as to the task ahead and the challenges confronting those who would carry forth His message of love. He warned them that they should be prepared for violent opposition; they would be like lambs amongst wolves. They should not expect universal acceptance; some people would receive them and their message, whilst others would refuse them.

Down through the centuries, prayer has been the powerhouse of God's work at home and abroad. Because saints have gathered together to pray, blessing has been enjoyed by the Lord's servants labouring thousands of miles away. The same prayer for labourers that the Lord encouraged then is just as urgent today.

Praying on the mountain and in the valley
The Lord Jesus not only spoke of a path of suffering but also He showed that there was glory ahead. On one occasion, taking three disciples with Him, He went up into a mountain to pray; as He was praying, He was transfigured (Lk 9.29). The scene was one of blinding glory at the presence of God; hence, there was a need for the cloud on that mountain.

Glory is but the manifestation of the divine presence and divine excellence. Throughout Scripture we catch glimpses of that glory and often it is linked with a cloud, for no one can look upon the face of God and live. That is the reason why Moses' request and prayer to God, "Shew me thy glory", could only be granted so long as he was hidden in a cleft of the rock and God covered Moses' face with His hand (Ex 33.18-23). When the children of Israel were journeying through the wilderness, a pillar of cloud guided them and also assured them of God's presence with them. On the Day of Atonement, when the high priest entered the innermost compartment of the tabernacle, the Holy of Holies, he had to have his hands full of incense.

When this was placed upon the fire he carried in a censer, a cloud covered the mercy seat and protected him; otherwise, he would have died (Lev 16.13).

Life has its mountaintop experiences but there are also valleys through which we must pass, dark moments when sorrow can overwhelm us and prayer is our only recourse. In the Garden of Gethsemane, the Saviour drew aside to kneel and pray concerning the cup of suffering that was to be His (Lk 22.39-46). His one desire was that the Father's will should be accomplished: "Nevertheless, not my will, but thine be done ... And being in an agony he prayed more earnestly: and his sweat was as it were great drops of blood falling down to the ground." Luke used four Greek words unique to the New Testament to record Christ's agony, earnestness, and bloodlike sweat. Sadly, during this deep trial of the Saviour, the disciples were fast asleep and unable to render any support.

Praying aright and praying wrongly
After watching the Saviour pray, one of the disciples approached Him with a request, "Lord, teach us to pray" (Lk 11.1). The Lord gave them all a model prayer. He taught them that they must first consider the greatness of God and His purposes; He is worthy of praise. Thereafter, they could turn to their own needs. The Lord knew that they would have a daily need of food; a frequent need of forgiveness; a constant need of vigilance and protection from evil. It was hardly the Lord's intention that they or we should make a practice of repeating the exact words by rote. Unfortunately, this seems to be the custom today, and the beautiful words have lost their edge on the lips of many, through thoughtless repetition.

The Lord continued to teach about prayer by narrating a parable unique to Luke's Gospel (Lk 11.5-13). In that story a friend came at a most inconvenient hour, begging for bread to feed an unexpected guest. His request was granted only because he was persistent. Another similar parable presented the pleas of a widow who also was shamelessly persistent in her asking (Lk 18.1-8). In these two stories, the Lord was emphasizing the need to ask, seek and knock, without giving up: "Men ought always to pray, and not to faint."

A third parable concerned two men who went up to the temple to pray (Lk 18.9-14). The Pharisee's prayer of self-righteous pride went unheard in heaven's courts whereas the publican's humble plea, as that of a penitent sinner, was welcomed and answered with the blessings of forgiveness and justification. The Pharisee's boastful monologue was described as "praying thus with himself". He was the only one who heard it; it was full of self. On the other hand, the despised publican had difficulty putting words together. He was deeply conscious of his own sin and cried out for mercy. His humble and sincere prayer reached the ear and the heart of God.

Praying for friends and enemies
We still find it remarkable that in His hour of deepest woe the Saviour could think of others, even those who had let Him down. Luke alone tells us of the Lord's words to Peter. Calling him "Simon", He warned him of the trial that lay ahead and the evil designs of Satan to target Peter and shake him to the core. There were also words of reassurance: "But I have prayed for thee, that thy faith fail not: and when thou art converted, strengthen thy brethren" (Lk 22.31-34). Peter, as usual, vigorously proclaimed his loyalty, but he was soon to deny his Lord three times. After his restoration, the words of Christ were indeed fulfilled, and in Peter's two letters we see how subsequently he wrote to strengthen those whose faith was being severely tested.

Of the seven sayings of Christ from the cross, one was a plea for His tormentors. This was perfectly in keeping with His earlier teaching: "Love your enemies, do good to them which hate you, bless them that curse you, and pray for them which despitefully use you" (Lk 6.27-28). He interceded on their behalf, praying repeatedly to the Father that they might be forgiven: "Father, forgive them; for they know not what they do" (Lk 23.34). Such was His great love for them. What they did know was that they had rejected a man called Jesus, but they refused to accept that He was God's Son and their Messiah. They were unaware of the consequences of their actions and the judgment they were bringing upon themselves.

After Christ rose from the dead and ascended to the Father's right hand, He did not stop praying. We are encouraged to know that He is in heaven today where He ever lives to make intercession for us (Heb 7.25).

A PERSONAL REMINDER
To become more like Christ, I must:
- speak often to the Father
- be thankful for everything
- be fervent in believing prayer.

CHAPTER 4

His Leading by the Spirit

The Lord Jesus moved through life in communion with His Father and under the control of the Holy Spirit. He was responsive to the Spirit's leading and guiding in all the circumstances of His life, and He served in the power of that same Spirit. We notice the influence of the Holy Spirit throughout His life.

His Forerunner

John the Baptist announced the coming of our Lord. John's ministry was aimed at preparing the hearts of the people to repent of their sins and to receive their Messiah. John's mother, Elisabeth, was filled by the Holy Spirit (Lk 1.41), as was John himself (Lk 1.15). When John spoke of the coming Messiah, he declared that He was mightier and worthier than himself. He also added that whereas he would baptize with water, Christ would baptize "with the Holy Ghost and with fire" (Mt 3.11; Mk 1.8; Lk 3.16). The baptism with the Holy Ghost took place when the Church began on the day of Pentecost and many believed the gospel. The baptism with fire referred to a separate and yet future day of judgment upon the unbelieving of earth.

His Conception

The Holy Spirit was at work in our Lord's conception so that Mary, a virgin, found herself expecting a child. The Scripture says, "She was found with child of the Holy Ghost" (Mt 1.18). When Joseph learned of this, he was determined that she should not be exposed to public shame, even though he was considering breaking off the engagement. (He had not had any physical relations with her.) At that critical time of doubt and distress, the angel appeared to him with words of explanation and reassurance: "that which is conceived in her is of the Holy Ghost" (Mt 1.20). To Mary herself came the revelation, "The Holy Ghost shall come upon thee, and the power of the Highest shall overshadow thee: therefore also that holy thing that shall be born of thee shall be called the Son of God" (Lk 1.35).

We have no reason to believe that the Lord's birth was anything other than a natural one; however, what was miraculous and supernatural was that it was a virgin who conceived. Her conception was by the Holy Spirit, and her child was divine: God manifest in the flesh.

The truth of our Lord's incarnation goes beyond our understanding but yet it remains a foundation of our faith. Had the Lord not been human, He could not have suffered, bled and died; had He not been divine, His death would have been insufficient to deal with the question of universal sin. In one person were both absolute deity and perfect humanity. We struggle to grasp this mystery with our limited comprehension. At present we can only cling to the fact of it and worship at the wonder of it. There is a day coming in heaven when we shall begin to understand more fully how it all came to be.

His Baptism

The Holy Spirit descended upon Christ when He was baptized by John in the Jordan River, just before He moved out into a public ministry. The people who were there that day received two signs: one was visible – the dove; the other was audible – the voice. The dove symbolized the Lord's purity, faithfulness and gentleness. God spoke from heaven concerning His beloved Son who had already pleased Him so well (Mt 3.17; Mk 1.11; Lk 3.22). During those quiet years in Nazareth, there would have been no shoddy workmanship and no 'seconds' for sale in that humble business; the simplest stool He constructed would have been a masterpiece. A change of ministry to a public sphere did not mean any change in attitude, for He always did those things which pleased the Father.

In Leviticus 2 we read of the meal offering, one of the voluntary offerings that an Israelite could bring to God for His pleasure. The four ingredients were fine flour, oil, salt and frankincense. In the act of offering it, the oil was poured upon the fine flour. This was a figure of the Lord's baptism when the Spirit descended upon the One whose life was pure, sinless and fragrant before God.

His Temptation
The same Spirit that anointed Christ then led Him to face the tempter (Mt 4.1-11; Mk 1.12-13; Lk 4.1-13). The temptation was not a surprise attack from the devil but a divine challenge to the enemy. The testing took place in a barren wilderness and Christ was full of the Holy Ghost when He arrived there (Lk 4.1). It was after forty days and nights of fasting that Satan came. In three subtle appeals the devil sought to draw away the Saviour from His solitary pathway of devotion to the will of God. Using the Scriptures like a sword, our Lord countered and rejected each appeal.

Following this encounter the devil was left the weaker. He would have had to acknowledge his inability on that occasion to divert the Son of God from His course. He would attack again and try other ways to overcome Christ, but in the end it was Christ who overcame him through His death at Calvary (Heb 2.14).

His Service
After the temptation, the Lord Jesus "returned in the power of the Spirit into Galilee: and there went out a fame of Him through all the region round about" (Lk 4.14). Many challenges to the Saviour's resolve still remained; He was confronted frequently by those possessed with either a single unclean spirit or at times

a great number of them (Mk 5.9). These spirits were the emissaries of Satan and took control of different individuals, being sometimes linked to physical infirmities such as deafness and dumbness (Mk 9.25).

Although we know that Satan is not omnipresent, the reality of evil everywhere is undeniably a result of his many ambassadors spreading his influence abroad. These angels who fell with him still do his bidding even to this day. Their judgment is already set, for the everlasting fire of hell has been prepared for them (Mt 25.41): they will not be spared.

The Lord refused to allow these unclean spirits to testify of Him, even though they knew who He was. In the synagogue in Capernaum, the unclean spirit afflicting one man spoke of the Lord as "Jesus of Nazareth …the Holy One of God" (Lk 4.34). This spirit was silenced before being commanded to come out of the man. And at the end of a busy day, after healing many, we read that "devils also came out of many, crying out, and saying, Thou art Christ the Son of God. And he rebuking them suffered them not to speak: for they knew that he was Christ" (Lk 4.41).

These incidents remind us that there is a battle raging in the spirit world. It is fierce and relentless. We may not see it, but we often feel it and have to contend and wrestle with it (Eph 6.12). Thank God, Christ is able to give us the victory; His power is all-prevailing.

Not only was Christ anointed and able to contend with the world of evil spirits, but also He had a glorious ministry that fulfilled the prophesy of Isaiah: "The Spirit of the Lord is upon me, because he hath anointed me to preach the gospel to the poor; he hath sent me to heal the brokenhearted, to preach deliverance to the captives, and recovering of sight to the blind, to set at liberty them that are bruised, to preach the acceptable year of the Lord" (Lk 4.18-19; Isa 61.1-2). His ministry was enriching, encouraging, liberating and enlightening, as He dealt with the ravages that sin had wrought.

Even the manner of His ministry and service was controlled by the Spirit, as noted earlier: "Behold my servant, whom I have chosen; my beloved, in whom my soul is well pleased: I will put my spirit upon him, and he shall shew judgment to the Gentiles. He shall not strive, nor cry; neither shall any man hear his voice in the streets. A bruised reed shall he not break, and smoking flax shall he not quench, till he send forth judgment unto victory" (Mt 12.18-20; Isa 42.1-3). The humility and gentleness of Christ are here described as well as His ultimate vindication and victory over all of His foes.

The Lord Jesus never moved outside the will of God, being always guided by the Holy Spirit. Unfortunately, we are still prone to take our own independent path and we can grieve the Spirit (Eph 4.30). This our Lord never did.

His Death and Resurrection
Time and again throughout Scripture we see the Father, Son and Holy Spirit working in harmony. Even before human life was created upon earth, the conference amongst the three persons of the Godhead came to this joint conclusion: "Let us make man in our image" (Gen 1.26). At the cross it was no different when Christ "through the eternal Spirit offered himself without spot to God" (Heb 9.14).

The work that Christ accomplished on the cross of Calvary has not only regained all that was lost through Adam's sin, but also has added much more. The One who gave human life in the beginning is the same One who is the source of eternal life now. We who were dead in our sins have been quickened and made alive through faith in Him. His voluntary sacrifice brought pleasure and satisfaction to God, and this is the everlasting theme of heaven's joy and praise. As for us too, the results of Christ's work are eternal: we have an eternal redemption and an eternal inheritance (Heb 9.12, 15).

The resurrection of Christ showed the approval of His Father. The early preachers of the gospel in the first century were bold and forthright in declaring to the Jews that they had killed the Son of God, but they were quick to add, God had raised him! (Acts 2.24, 32; 3.15, 26; 4.10; 5.30). The work of resurrection was attributed to the Holy Spirit. Christ was "declared to be the Son of God with power, according to the spirit of holiness, by the resurrection from the dead" (Rom 1.4). It is the Holy Spirit who "raised up Jesus from the dead" (Rom 8.11). Peter says that Christ was "put to death in the flesh, but quickened by the Spirit" (1 Pet 3.18).

After the resurrection, Christ appeared only to His own "until the day in which he was taken up, after that he through the Holy Ghost had given commandments unto the apostles whom he had chosen" (Acts 1.2). His ministry immediately after the resurrection was in the power of the Spirit. Even now His present ministry in communicating with His church is through the same Spirit (Rev 2.7).

His Teaching
The best known teaching that Christ gave concerning the Holy Spirit is found in John's Gospel. (We need to range over several chapters to extract the relevant truths.) It seems that He did not present the truth as a single subject but wove the various strands of it throughout His remarks. He met with eleven of the disciples in an upper room in Jerusalem where He sought to prepare and strengthen their hearts before leaving them (Jn 13-17). He explained that if He did not go, the Spirit would not come, but after leaving them He would send the Comforter to be with them (Jn 16.7).

This beautiful title of the Holy Spirit, "the Comforter", was used four times by the Lord Jesus. When He spoke of the Spirit as "another Comforter", He meant that the Spirit would be another just like Himself. The original word describes someone called to our side to help us in our need. Christ was reassuring them that in His physical absence they were not being abandoned. His own Spirit would be there, not just beside them but dwelling within them; and not just for a time, but for ever (Jn 14.16-18). The Holy Spirit was active upon earth during our Lord's ministry but after the Lord's departure and return to heaven, His work upon earth was continued by the same Spirit.

The Holy Spirit indwells every new believer from the moment of conversion. He is our Lord's seal of ownership upon us and the guarantee of the blessings to come (Eph 1.13-14). He witnesses to our own spirits that we are the sons of God, and He also assists us in our prayers when at times we hardly know how to pray as we ought (Rom 8.16, 26).

Christ taught that the Holy Spirit, "whom the Father will send in my name", would teach them all things and remind them of what Christ had said to them (Jn 14.26). These truths, the teachings of Christ, are found today in the four *Gospels*. He, the Spirit of truth, would testify to them concerning their absent Lord (Jn 15.26).

Christ also told them that when the Holy Spirit came He would convict the world of sin, of righteousness and future judgment (Jn 16.8). Following Christ's return to glory, the disciples waited in Jerusalem for the coming of the Holy Spirit. After this took place on the day of Pentecost, they were empowered and emboldened to go forth and proclaim the good news of the gospel to others. Like ever widening ripples in a lake, the message was carried further and further afield. They began by witnessing in Jerusalem, but soon the word spread to Judaea, Samaria and unto the uttermost part of the earth. That work continues to this day. The record of the exploits of those first witnesses and preachers is found primarily in the book of the *Acts*.

The Lord further taught that the Spirit would guide them into all truth and also show them things to come (Jn 16.13). These are the things that the remaining books of the New Testament, the *Epistles* and the *Revelation*, bring before us. Indeed, the Spirit of God and the complete Word of God are complementary in enlightening us as to God's will for us and then empowering us to fulfil it.

The Spirit of God has continued to accomplish in believers what Christ began when He was upon earth. The disciples had the comfort of Christ's physical presence with them and now we have the presence of His Comforter, the indwelling Spirit. The Lord taught His followers the truth of God, and now the Spirit reminds us of those same words and helps us to understand them. Christ directly challenged those who needed salvation and today the Spirit convicts sinners of their sin, God's righteousness, and judgment to come.

The Holy Spirit will always direct attention to the person of Christ and glorify Him (Jn 16.14). When we are controlled by the Spirit of God, we will do the same. We will exalt and make much of God's Son. And when we seek to be empty of self, the Spirit can fill us so that we become more like Christ and bear the fruit of the Spirit (Gal 5.22-23). He reproduces Christ in us.

A PERSONAL REMINDER
To become more like Christ, I must:
- be filled with the Holy Spirit
- be led and guided by Him
- rely upon His power in service.

CHAPTER 5

His Obedience to the Word

It should not surprise us that the Lord Jesus knew the Scriptures so well: after all, He was the author of them. When He was challenged by the Sadducees with a seemingly difficult question concerning the marriage relationship after death, He replied, "Ye do err, not knowing the scriptures, nor the power of God" (Mt 22.29). In this short reply we have two important truths: firstly, for us to know the mind and will of God we need to know the Scriptures; secondly, spiritual understanding of the Word of God comes only to those who are acquainted with the Author and know His power in their lives.

Our Lord's Bible
The Bible used by the Lord would have been quite different from ours today in its physical form, content and arrangement. The Scriptures existed then as handwritten papyrus or leather scrolls. They contained the books of the Old Testament arranged in three sections – the Law, the Prophets and the Writings (the last of these included the Psalms). The New Testament had not yet been written.

In the synagogue in Nazareth, Christ was handed an Isaiah scroll which He unrolled until He found the appropriate place for His reading (Lk 4.16-18). On the Sabbath day it was the Jewish custom that the first lesson be made up of several readings from the Law; the second lesson comprised a reading from the Prophets. The Lord led this second lesson and it is likely that this public reading in the synagogue was in the original Hebrew. In further discourses He quoted extensively from the Greek version of the Old Testament, the Septuagint, which was in wide circulation at that time.

The division of the Scriptures into three major sections was reflected in the conversation that Christ conducted with two downhearted believers on the road to Emmaus after His resurrection: "And beginning at Moses and all the prophets, he expounded unto them in all the scriptures the things concerning himself"; "These are the words which I spake unto you, while I was yet with you, that all things must be fulfilled, which were written in the law of Moses, and in the prophets, and in the psalms, concerning me. Then opened he their understanding, that they might understand the scriptures" (Lk 24.27, 44-45).

Christ quoted directly from every section of the Old Testament and He also alluded to many other biblical incidents and characters. These are too numerous to mention here, but one is left with the conclusion that the Lord was totally familiar with all aspects of the Scriptures. He knew what had happened and had been recorded in the past and its significance for the hearers of His own time (and for us even today).

The Prophetic Scriptures

Christ was conscious of the need to fulfil all that had been written in the Scriptures concerning His coming to earth and His ministry amongst men. There were references to Him in all of the three divisions of the Hebrew Scriptures, but it was the prophetic writers particularly who had much to say concerning His coming. The prophet had a two-fold function: he boldly told forth the truth and he also foretold the future. The first meant that he had a specific message for his own day which he proclaimed faithfully. He challenged the people and when, as often was the case, they had strayed far from God, he urged them to return in repentance to the Lord. Then, secondly, he had a message of prediction for Israel. It could be for the near future – something that could happen to them in their own lifetime, such as the time of their captivity and restoration – or it could have a more distant time frame, particularly concerning the return of the Lord to earth to set up His millennial kingdom.

The prophets saw, as it were, only two mountain peaks concerning the Messiah's coming. There was His first coming to earth in lowliness and humility to die upon a cross; then there was His second coming to earth in power and glory, to destroy His enemies and set up His earthly kingdom. What the prophets did not see was the valley between the two peaks: the time of this present Church age, ending with what we call 'the Rapture', when the Lord returns to the air to catch away those who have been saved in this period of grace. All of this was hidden from their view.

One challenge to our reading and understanding of the Old Testament Scriptures concerning Christ is that His two comings to earth can be referred to within the space of only a few phrases and with no obvious break between. An example might make the matter clearer: in Isaiah 53.10 we read, "Yet it pleased the Lord to bruise him; he hath put him to grief: when thou shalt make his soul an offering for sin, he shall see his seed, he shall prolong his days, and the pleasure of the Lord shall prosper in his hand." Clearly, the first half of the verse speaks of Christ's sufferings and grief upon the cross. The second half speaks of a coming time of pleasure and prosperity. We must always ask ourselves, "Which of the comings is being referred to in this phrase? Is it His coming to die as the Saviour or His coming to reign as the King?" Hopefully, we can see that both of His comings are in view in the verse above. Apply this test to another verse from Isaiah: "For unto us a child is born, unto us a son is given: and the government shall be upon his shoulder" (Isa 9.6). Is Christ's first coming being referred to, or is it His second coming, or both?

When He was here upon earth, Christ knew that all the Scriptures concerning His first coming would be fulfilled. As we shall see, they were all carried out exactly to the letter. This is an assurance to us that the promises of Scripture that remain will also be fulfilled; God is still on the throne and He is working out His eternal purposes according to His will. We need not have any doubts or fears about the future.

The Fulfilment of Scripture in His Life

The Gospel recorded by Matthew forms a bridge between the Old and the New Testaments. Matthew showed that Christ was the promised Messiah, the King of the Jews. The spiritual leaders and the people should have recognized this. He had a royal lineage (ch 1); a unique birth (ch 2); and a forerunner (ch 3) who prepared the way for His public ministry. His character was impeccable (ch 4); His teachings were incomparable (ch 5-7); His power was indisputable (ch 8-9). The sad outcome was that the nation rejected their king and from chapter 10 onwards, we see a rising tide of ridicule, scorn and hatred, ending with Christ being nailed to a cross.

Matthew proved that the early events surrounding Christ's birth and infancy were in keeping with Scripture: "And she shall bring forth a son, and thou shalt call his name Jesus: for he shall save his people from their sins. Now all this was done, *that it might be fulfilled* [all italics mine] which was spoken of the Lord by the prophet, saying, Behold, a virgin shall be with child, and shall bring forth a son, and they shall call his name Emmanuel, which being interpreted is, God with us" (Mt 1.21-23; Isa 7.14); "And when he [Herod] had gathered all the chief priests and scribes of the people together, he demanded of them where Christ should be born. And they said unto him, In Bethlehem of Judaea: *for thus it is written* by the prophet, And thou Bethlehem, in the land of Judah, art not the least among the princes of Judah: for out of thee shall come a Governor, that shall rule my people Israel" (Mt 2.4-6; Mic 5.2); "When he [Joseph] arose, he took the young child and his mother by night, and departed into Egypt: And was there until the death of Herod: *that it might be fulfilled* which was spoken of the Lord by the prophet, saying, Out of Egypt have I called my son" (Mt 2.14-15; Hos 11.1).

When Christ was about thirty years of age, He moved out into a public ministry. When He healed those who were sick, He was fulfilling prophetic Scriptures: "When the even was come, they brought unto him many that were possessed with devils: and he cast out the spirits with his word, and healed all that were sick: *That it might be fulfilled* which was spoken by Esaias the prophet, saying, Himself took our infirmities, and bare our sicknesses" (Mt 8.16-17; Isa 53.4). The quiet manner of His ministry too was in keeping with what had been foretold (Mt 12.15-21; Isa 42.1-4). In His teaching ministry, Christ often used parables as a way of communicating truth to those who were willing to hear it, but at the same time, concealing truth from those who were habitually resisting it. The prophet, Isaiah, had foretold this also (Mt 13.13-17; Isa 6.9-10).

Christ's first words recorded in Matthew's Gospel were spoken just before His baptism, when He referred to the fulfilling of righteousness (Mt 3.15). He knew that the things which had been promised or anticipated had to be carried out in full. After John baptized Him, He was led by the Spirit into the wilderness to be tempted by the devil. Over the next three years He would bring blessing to many, but opposition to His person and resistance to His teaching were never far away.

As the storm clouds of final rejection gathered, Christ drew near to Jerusalem, fully conscious that the manner of His entry into the city was in accordance with Scripture (Mt 21.1-11; Zec 9.9). The crowd joyously welcomed Him but soon others would be railing against Him and baying for His blood. The treachery of Judas too was instrumental in initiating the arrest and mock trial before the crucifixion. The Lord said to His disciples when He was arrested, "How then shall the scriptures be fulfilled, that thus it must be? ... But all this was done *that the scriptures of the prophets might be fulfilled*" (Mt 26.54, 56). The thirty pieces of silver had been foretold, as had the shameful act of casting lots for His garments after He was nailed to the tree (Mt 27.1-10, 35-36; Zec 11.12-13; Ps 22.17-18).

The other Gospel writers also freely quoted the Old Testament as foretelling different events in Christ's life but none as extensively as Matthew. His Gospel should have had a special appeal to the Jews but they preferred the darkness of their own pride to the light of God's Word. Barabbas or even Caesar was preferred to their own Messiah. At least Pilate was bold enough to uphold the truth when he wrote a title proclaiming that Jesus was the King of the Jews (Mt 27.37). The chief priests wanted him to change the writing to say that these words were only a personal claim of the man, Jesus, rather than a fact. Pilate refused (Jn 19.19-22).

The Declaration of Scripture in His Words

Christ not only quoted Scripture, but He also spoke Scripture. His words went forth with divine authority and that is why we have so many of His conversations and teaching discourses recorded for us in the New Testament. In the truest sense, these inspired words have been 'God-breathed'.

At times Christ indicated that He, as the obedient Son, was passing on the words of His Father. In the teaching given to His disciples in the upper room, He told them that, "all things that I have heard of my Father I have made known unto you" (Jn 15.15). In His prayer to the Father He was able to declare that, "I have given unto them the words which thou gavest me …I have given them thy word" (Jn 17.8, 14).

At other times He spoke with conviction as to His own words. Some argue that the Law given to Moses represents God's unalterable standard; the words of the Lord Jesus taught an even higher standard. Under grace it is not enough to keep to the letter of the law, but we must rise higher and because of love fulfil the spirit of the law. Five times over Christ spoke in

this way: "Ye have heard that it was said by them of old time …
but I say unto you…" (Mt 5.21-22, 27-28, 33-34, 38-39, 43-44). It
may be that we have never killed anyone, but still we have
harboured murderous thoughts; we may have avoided the sin
of adultery, yet burned with lust; we may love our friends, but
never have sought to love our enemies. This was the challenge
of His words.

When they came to arrest Him in the garden, He went to meet
them and asked them who it was they were seeking? When
they replied that they were seeking Jesus of Nazareth, He
identified Himself as the "I am". This unexpected reply – one
of the exclusive titles of Almighty God (Ex 3.14) – stunned them,
and they fell to the ground. Christ's self-confessed identity as
the Son of God was the thing that had so often incensed the
Jews; they refused to accept His claim and charged Him with
blasphemy.

In John's Gospel there are seven well known occurrences of
our Lord's claims to be the eternal and unchanging "I am".
Through faith in Christ alone every believer has come into the
good of receiving salvation and eternal life: "I am the door …
by me if any man enter in, He shall be saved"; I am the way, the
truth and the life, no man cometh unto the Father but by me"
(Jn 10.10; 14.6). To sustain us on the journey home, He feeds us
and satisfies our souls: "I am the bread of life" (Jn 6.35). To
guide us on the pathway, He illuminates the darkness: "I am
the light of the world" (Jn 8.12). To enable us to bear fruit, He
nourishes us: "I am the true vine" (Jn 15.1). To care for us always
and protect us, He holds us securely in His hand: "I am the
good shepherd" (Jn 10.11,28). To fulfil our hopes beyond the
grave, He gives us reassurance: "I am the resurrection and the
life" (Jn 11.25). This ongoing revelation of Christ is a great
strength and comfort to us who believe. The written Word
became the living Word and in Christ, God has drawn near to
us. The truth of all of His claims can be affirmed in our lives
day by day.

The Application of Scripture to our Lives

Christ exhorted the disciples to keep His commandments and thereby show their love for Him – their obedience was important to Him. In the Gospel of John He challenged them, "If ye love me keep my commandments" (Jn 14.15); "If a man love me, he will keep my words: and my Father will love him, and we will come unto him, and make our abode with him" (Jn 14.23).

We sometimes twist and turn to avoid simple obedience. King Saul made elaborate excuses when he was confronted with his disobedience in sparing king Agag. God had commanded that the Amalekites and their livestock be utterly destroyed. Instead, the Israelites had kept Agag alive and offered their animals as sacrifices. Samuel had to tell Saul that, "to obey is better than sacrifice, and to hearken than the fat of rams" (1 Sam 15.22).

May we be simple enough and wise enough to take heed to Mary's advice concerning the words of Christ: at the wedding in Cana of Galilee she told the servants, "Whatsoever he saith unto you, do it" (Jn 2.5).

> *A PERSONAL REMINDER*
> To become more like Christ, I must:
> • listen daily to God's voice in His Word
> • seek to understand it
> • obey it.

CHAPTER 6

His Thoughts and Emotions

What are the driving forces that motivate people today? What makes them tick? What do they think about most? For millions of poor people in the third world, the daily grind is dominated by one principal thought: "Where is my next meal coming from?" They are preoccupied with scraping together a living for themselves and their families, simply to survive. Most of us who are accustomed to more favourable circumstances know very little about such poverty and need.

There are other forces that come into play and dominate the minds of many in more favoured societies today. People think chiefly about themselves and what they want. At the risk of being simplistic, we might say that they are motivated by the desire for at least one (or a combination) of four things – position, power, prosperity and pleasure.

There are those who spend vast sums of money to win high public office and then expend as much effort trying to stay there for as long as possible. They would have us believe that they do it for our benefit alone. Others of a more ruthless nature stage coups, not all of them bloodless. Politicians and dictators strut on the world stage just like Nebuchadnezzar did long ago. The power they wield affects everyone else beneath them but eventually, having had their brief day of glory, they must pass on. The same kind of scenario is played out in a smaller scale at all levels of society, as people seek to promote and advance themselves over others.

Some, who are not necessarily attracted by power and position, cannot resist the desire to acquire personal wealth. By fair means or foul they seek to accumulate more and more money; the lure of riches is as strong today as it ever was, whether in capitalistic societies or communistic societies. People want more and more things, believing that this is the path to happiness, but they end up being even more miserable.

What of the pleasure principle? We do not have to look far to find it in operation. There are those who live for the weekend and the ritual binge of drinking, partying and all that goes with it. The underlying philosophy of our age is self-centred, focused on the present, and increasingly antagonistic to God and His Word.

The revealed thoughts of Christ are completely different. They refresh us and come as pure, cold water to thirsty souls. Some of the things He taught as to life itself, true greatness and true joy, might at first seem to be paradoxical; nevertheless, they are all true.

His Thoughts on Position
One day a woman a mother brought her two sons before the Saviour with the request that they be given prominent seats in the coming kingdom. Specifically, she had in mind that one should sit on the right hand immediately beside the Saviour and the other on the left hand, but she gave no reasons why her sons should merit such special favour. The Lord corrected her lack of understanding, reminding her of the path of suffering that He must first tread before He would take His own place in the kingdom. Then He informed her that the Father alone could grant such privileges (Mt 20.20-28).

An unchanging divine principle was then explained: the way to be great is to serve others. In God's estimation, the way down is the way up, paradoxical as it may appear. It is the opposite in the world where men constantly seek position to rule others.

To drive the point home, the Lord spoke of His own coming into the world to be a lowly servant and eventually to give His life for others.

On another occasion, Christ had been telling His disciples of His coming arrest, death and resurrection. They did not understand this nor even ask for clarification. They were concerned about a more pressing matter: "Who should be the greatest?" When their Master enquired as to the topic of their conversation, it seems that they were ashamed to own up. Christ knew, of course. Again He sought to correct their worldly thinking: "If any man desire to be first, the same shall be last of all, and servant of all" (Mk 9.31-37). To illustrate this lesson, he took a little child up in His arms and explained that those who received such were, in fact, receiving Him.

In the upper room in Jerusalem, before His arrest and crucifixion, He took something else to teach the same truth: He reached for a towel with which He girded Himself. After pouring water into a basin of water, He stooped down and began to wash the disciples' feet. When that was over He sat down with them and told them what it meant: "If I then, your Lord and Master, have washed your feet; ye also ought to wash one another's feet. For I have given you an example, that ye should do as I have done to you. Verily, verily, I say unto you, The servant is not greater than his lord; neither he that is sent greater than he that sent him. If ye know these things, happy are ye if ye do them" (Jn 13.14-17). The road to blessing meant following His example and serving others. He promised joy to those who would take up this challenge.

His Thoughts on Power
God is on the side of the big battalions – so say many. The superpowers are all anxious to be able to outgun each other; and so the arms race continues unabated, only now there are new contestants who have entered the competition. What is the believer to make of it all? Should we be worried? No! We

need have no worries at all for our Lord is still on the throne and He it is who rules over the kingdoms of men and sets their boundaries. Pilate had said to Christ, "Knowest thou not that I have power to crucify thee, and have power to release thee? Jesus answered, Thou couldest have no power at all against me, except it were given thee from above" (Jn 19.10-11). One day Christ's power will be fully manifested and His greatness will be acknowledged by all.

When the enemies of Christ came to arrest Him in the garden, Peter instinctively drew his sword and wielded it, injuring the servant of the high priest. The Lord commanded him to return it to its sheath, saying, "Put up again thy sword into his place: for all they that take the sword shall perish with the sword" (Mt 26.52). He had earlier told Pilate, "My kingdom is not of this world: if my kingdom were of this world, then would my servants fight, that I should not be delivered to the Jews: but now is my kingdom not from hence" (Jn 18.36).

As they bound Him and led Him away, He went meekly. It looked as if He was just caving in to their evil designs; He seemed a passive victim, not least when they nailed Him to a cross and began to taunt and mock Him. In love He prayed for His tormentors. But what seemed to be the greatest defeat turned out to be the most magnificent victory in the history of this planet. That day Christ completed a work that has brought eternal life and liberty to millions. He dealt the decisive blow to the devil by annulling his power. He overcame sin by becoming the sacrifice for it. He defeated death when on the third day He arose triumphant from the grave. Now He lives in the power of an endless life.

Servants we may be and weak at the best, but we are in touch with the Almighty. The weapons of our warfare are not carnal but spiritual. Through the unseen power of even our feeblest prayers, God's blessings can flow out to others. Through the sowing of seeds of truth from the living Word of God, there springs up an abundant and enduring harvest. Through the demonstration of the divine love which has first been shed abroad in our own hearts, other hearts can be touched as well.

His Thoughts on Prosperity

The Lord Jesus lived out what He taught. He owned very little. When He died there were only a few items of clothing to be distributed amongst common soldiers. There was no unseemly scrabble for anything else of value in worldly terms. For over three years He had journeyed throughout Galilee, Judaea and Samaria, supported by the kindness of those who followed Him and loved Him. From time to time He borrowed things such as a boat, a donkey and a coin. Certain homes were open to Him where He found care and companionship. He had no home of His own: "And every man went unto his own house. Jesus went unto the mount of Olives" (Jn 7.53-8.1).

In His teaching He warned of the dangers of wealth and spelt out how many rich people would have difficulty in making spiritual or heavenly things a priority: "How hardly shall they that have riches enter into the kingdom of God!" (Mk 10.23). Riches bring a false sense of security, satisfaction and well-being. They make people feel self-sufficient and cause them to act independently of God and others. The truth is that riches can cheat us with their deceitfulness and strangle any real desire for spiritual things.

God has had His rich men like Joseph of Arimathaea who have used their wealth for the blessing of others. The rich man of Luke 16 who died and went to hell was not being penalized for being rich: His mistake was that he had given no thought to his eternal welfare and he had to leave all of his wealth behind, as all men must. There had been nothing for God in his life.

His Thoughts on Pleasure

Running after pleasure is an exercise in vanity for it will always escape those who long for it the most. King Solomon learnt the hard way that the pleasures of this world can never satisfy the soul. He tried every avenue to find satisfaction but only ended up declaring that it was all in vain (Ecc 12.8).

The Lord Jesus knew the secret of true and lasting joy. The psalmist spoke prophetically of Him when he wrote, "I delight to do thy will, O my God: yea, thy law is within my heart" (Ps 40.8). Christ confessed that His meat was "to do the will of him that sent me, and to finish his work" (Jn 4.34). His eye was on the glory that lay ahead, "who for the joy that was set before him endured the cross, despising the shame" (Heb 12.2).

In summary, the teaching of Christ revealed His thinking and philosophy of life: not seeking position but seeking to serve; not pursuing power for selfish goals but using it for the blessing of others; not grasping but giving; not focused upon one's own pleasure but committed to serving God and fulfilling His will.

His Emotions
Christ experienced a full range of human emotions, sin apart. He had neither a cool nor detached approach to life and He knew nothing of 'a stiff upper lip'. The plight of individuals touched Him deeply and He responded with an intensity none of us has ever known. His prior knowledge of human circumstances never blunted His response and His frequent addressing of human need never caused Him to become casual or unfeeling.

We are so different. Many of us have been brought up in a culture which discourages the display of emotions. Not only do we recoil from the frothy emotionalism of some extreme religious groups, but also we struggle with any hint of emotion at all and are embarrassed should someone wear his heart on his sleeve. We can also hold back from becoming too deeply involved with the needs and suffering of others. There is an element of self-protection in this: empathy with human need is draining and sometimes we feel that we have reached our limit when sharing in another's grief or pain. As we shall see, the Saviour never shielded Himself from identifying fully with others.

So what was it that evoked His pleasure or pain? Why did he sometimes commend and at other times condemn? A number of explicit references in the Gospels to the emotions of Christ open up for us a window into His soul.

His Pleasure

The Lord "rejoiced" to see men and women exercising faith in God. As noted earlier, in a short prayer He thanked the Father, the Lord of heaven and earth, that He had revealed truth to those who were willing to receive it in childlike dependence and humble faith (Lk 10.21). By contrast, those who looked to their own worldly wisdom and knowledge could never become the recipients of divine truth.

The faith of a centurion also pleased Christ: He "marvelled" at the soldier's nobility in caring for his servant, his humility in declaring his own unworthiness and his trust in coming to the Lord for help. His faith contrasted with an unbelieving nation (Mt 8.5-13). The centurion and the nation would receive their appropriate rewards.

His Pain

Christ was deeply disturbed by unbelief and hypocrisy. Mark tells us that He was "angry" and felt "grief" at the hardness of the Pharisees' hearts (Mk 3.5), and He "sighed deeply" when they called for a sign (Mk 8.12). He knew that they were insincere. They sought only to tempt Him and then accuse Him, so that finally they might destroy Him. One of the three occasions the Saviour "wept" was when He lamented the unbelief of the inhabitants of Jerusalem. They had stubbornly refused to heed His tender pleadings (Lk 19.41).

Apart from the attitudes and actions of Christ's enemies, He was also "much displeased" with His own disciples when they rebuked those who brought their children to Him (Mk 10.14). How He loved the little ones! He drew them close to Himself, took them up in His arms and blessed them. Insensitivity and impatience were foreign to Him.

His Compassion

Whenever Christ met human need, He was "moved with compassion". He saw vast companies with no bread (Mt 14.14; 15.32) and lost souls with no shepherd (Mk 6.34). His heart went out to a leper who had no hope because of his disease (Mk 1.41) and a widow who had no hope because of the death of her boy (Lk 7.13). At the grave of Lazarus, His beloved friend, He "groaned" and "wept" (Jn 11.33). The last word indicates a silent weeping. He "loved" a young ruler who had seemed so zealous to inherit eternal life (Mk 10.21). Into these dire circumstances Christ brought food, care and healing, life, light and love. Only the rich ruler departed unblessed but certainly not unloved; other things were claiming his heart.

The exercise of divine power was not inconsequential to the Lord. When the woman with the issue of blood touched the hem of His garment, He knew that virtue had gone out of Him (Mk 5.30). He was not exhausted by this miracle nor was His power depleted; however, He was aware that the blessing had flowed out from Him. And still it flows today.

His Cup

Calvary overshadowed the Saviour's life. As a boy He was aware of His identity and responsibility: "I must be about my Father's business" (Lk 2.49). In later life He declared that He was "straitened" until His baptism would be accomplished (Lk 12.50). He was not thinking of being immersed in the Jordan but of being hung upon a cross. Luke's language indicates the weight of responsibility and the pain and distress He felt as He anticipated the waves of judgment that lay ahead.

As His appointed time drew near His soul was "troubled" (Jn 12.27). We see Him prostrate and lonely in the Garden of Gethsemane and we are permitted to be wondering spectators of His "agony" and His "strong crying and tears" (Lk 22.44; Heb 5.7). All the references to our Lord's tears indicate that these were shed in the vicinity of the Mount of Olives; however, this last mention does not refer to silent tears but to heart-rending cries of anguish. He was "exceeding sorrowful", "sore amazed" and "very heavy" (Mk 14.33-34; Mt 26.37) as He contemplated becoming the Sin-bearer. The suffering and shame, the hatred and pain, were only a prelude to the mighty onslaught of God's wrath that fell upon Him because of sin. The darkness was riven by the terrible cry, "My God, my God, why hast thou forsaken me?" (Mt 27.46). There was no answer: others in the past had appealed to God and found help, but He found none.

A Christian tourist was visiting in the Far East. He was led inside the vast hollow image of a heathen deity where he stood looking around. Finally, he gazed upwards and remarked, "It is truly magnificent, but I see no heart here" – no heart, no feelings, no love, no emotion. We can rejoice that the One we own as Lord remains supreme, "the sympathizing Jesus".

A PERSONAL REMINDER
To become more like Christ, I must:
- think of God and others before myself
- fix my mind and heart on heavenly interests
- be wholehearted in all that I do for Him.

CHAPTER 7

His Trials and Sufferings

The Lord Jesus suffered in more ways than we will ever know or understand. Because He was holy and pure, He must often have been affronted by the ugliness of sin in His close interactions with sinners. For over thirty years He lived in close contact with all kinds of people, some of whom were merely indifferent while others were openly antagonistic towards Him. He was also hounded by a relentless enemy, the devil, who tried by every means to tarnish Him, divert Him and overcome Him. In the end it was Satan who was defeated and his power overcome.

Tempted

We have already alluded to this early encounter with Satan, but now we consider further details of Christ's temptation in the Judaean wilderness. To this day it presents to the traveller a barren, rocky and inhospitable landscape; few tourists venture out of their buses to spend long there. By contrast, when Adam and Eve were tempted in the Garden of Eden, they were surrounded by beautiful greenness and lushness. In such a favourable environment they had all the physical comforts they could ever have needed; nevertheless, they still failed to withstand the enemy. Heeding the devil's voice, they fell headlong into sin.

Although the devil is subtle, his frequent attacks run along three well established lines, targeting body, soul and spirit: "For all that is in the world, the lust of the flesh, and the lust of the eyes, and the pride of life, is not of the Father, but is of the world" (1 Jn 2.16). All of these elements were involved in the temptation of our first parents. When Eve saw that "the tree was good for food [the lust of the flesh], and that it was pleasant to the eyes [the lust of the eyes], and a tree to be desired to make one wise [the pride of life], she took of the fruit thereof, and did eat, and gave also unto her husband with her; and he did eat" (Gen 3.6).

Christ was led into the wilderness by the Holy Spirit. After forty days and nights of fasting and in a weakened physical state, the comfort of an easy meal would have had a special appeal to the flesh. Satan urged Him to use His divine power to make stones into bread for His own needs. The Lord answered without hesitation, quoting from the book of Deuteronomy: "Man shall not live by bread alone but by every word that proceedeth from the mouth of God" (Lk 4.3-4; Deut 8.3).

The temptation that followed would have appealed to the eyes. Leaving the plain, they moved to a high mountain. From that vantage point the devil showed Christ all the kingdoms of the world in a moment of time, as if he, the devil, owned them and they were at his disposal. Satan had overcome Adam in the Garden of Eden and wrested control from him to become the prince of this world. He was now bargaining in the hope of procuring an act of worship from the Lord. Christ refused again and quoted another short passage from Deuteronomy: "Get thee behind me, Satan: for it is written, Thou shalt worship the Lord thy God, and him only shalt thou serve" (Lk 4.5-8; Deut 6.13).

The final assault was conducted from the pinnacle of the temple in Jerusalem. The devil challenged Christ with a kind of dare, to cast Himself down and let the angels rescue Him. Such a spectacular stunt would have appealed to pride. The devil quoted from a psalm, "He shall give his angels charge over thee, to keep thee: And in their hands they shall bear thee up, lest at any time thou dash thy foot against a stone" (Ps 91.11-12; Lk

4.9-12). The Lord countered this challenge with a third quotation from the book of Deuteronomy: "Thou shalt not tempt the Lord thy God" (Deut 6.16).

We observe that the devil quoted the Scriptures, but only with an evil intent. Many people are skilled in throwing quotations (sometimes misquotations) backwards and forwards only to advance their own ideas. The whole tone and teaching of Scripture must always be taken into account, and that is why a spiritual understanding – not merely an intellectual knowledge – is vital for us all.

The perfect sinlessness and true humanity of Christ fitted Him to be our Saviour. Deity cannot sin but is deeply affected by every challenge that sin presents. It was no small thing for Christ to be assaulted by the devil as he sought to divert Him from the path of selfless obedience to the Father.

The account of the Son of God and His forty days in the wilderness of Judaea contrasted with the history of Israel as they wandered for forty years in the wilderness of Sinai. They lusted after the food of Egypt and grew tired of God's provision of manna; they turned aside from worshipping God and fell into idolatry and immorality; they also doubted God's ability to protect them even though He rescued them time and again. Their frequent complaints were an insult and provocation to God.

Paul took up the example of Israel's history when he warned the Corinthians against carelessness and pride. He put it like this: "we should not lust after evil things, as they also lusted. Neither be ye idolaters, as were some of them … neither let us tempt Christ, as some of them also tempted, and were destroyed of serpents. Neither murmur ye, as some of them also murmured, and were destroyed of the destroyer" (1 Cor 10.6-10). The Israelites were overthrown in the wilderness, whereas Christ came forth victorious over the destroyer.

The threefold temptation in the wilderness was not the end of Satan's efforts to oppose Christ, as we have noted previously. The Scriptures tell us that the devil departed from Him "for a season" (Lk 4.13); there were further assaults in a concerted campaign against Him. When Christ spoke to the disciples about His sufferings that lay ahead, Peter hastily rebuked Him. The Lord well knew the source of Peter's words and He responded immediately and forthrightly: "Get thee behind me, Satan: for thou savourest not the things that be of God, but the things that be of men" (Mk 8.33). What a victory would have been gained by the devil, and what a fate would have been ours, if the Lord Jesus Christ had been turned away from the path of obedience!

Thirty years earlier, the same satanic source had been behind the plot to kill the Saviour when Herod planned to murder the infant King. Even long before that, there were other attempts to destroy or corrupt the royal seed in the line of Christ (2 Kgs 11.1-3). These were Satan's many efforts to "bruise" and wipe out the seed of the woman (Gen 3.15), and frustrate the purposes of God. Christ told the Pharisees, "But now ye seek to kill me … Ye do the deeds of your father … Ye are of your father the devil, and the lusts of your father ye will do. He was a murderer from the beginning, and abode not in truth" (Jn 8.40-44). Their evil plans were carried out in the name of religion and orthodoxy. Little has changed: religious extremism still drives some to commit gross atrocities and bloodshed. The psalmist had seen prophetically that the world and its leaders would have no time for God and His Son: "The kings of the earth set themselves, and the rulers take counsel together, against the Lord, and against his anointed, saying, Let us break their bands asunder, and cast away their cords from us" (Ps 2.2-3).

Towards the end of the Lord's life, when the mob led by Judas came to arrest Him, He reminded them, "I was daily with you in the temple, ye stretched forth no hands against me:

but this is your hour, and the power of darkness" (Lk 22.53). It was a dark hour indeed, and motivated by the prince of darkness.

Misunderstood

We normally expect our family and friends to understand us and lend encouragement, especially in a time of need. The Lord Jesus must have been disappointed when His own family and friends fell short on this. Apart from not understanding things He had taught them and shown them, they sometimes forgot what He said. On other occasions their faith was small and they failed to trust Him.

When Jesus was only twelve years old, Mary and Joseph took Him to Jerusalem for the Passover feast. When they were on their way back home, they did not realize at first that He had remained behind. On discovering this, they returned in haste and eventually they found Him sitting in the temple precincts amongst the learned men. Mary's words betrayed her agitation and feelings that Jesus had been inconsiderate: "Son, why hast thou thus dealt with us? Behold, thy father and I have sought thee sorrowing?" He replied, "How is it that ye sought me? wist ye not that I must be about my Father's business? And they understood not the sayings which he spake unto them" (Lk 2.41-51); however, Mary did not forget what He said but kept these sayings in her heart. As for the rest of His family, they did not believe in Him (Jn 7.5).

The disciples too were often dull concerning spiritual things. When the Lord spoke to them, they did not understand or, at times, even remember what He had said. In Galilee, He told them that He would die at the hands of violent men but rise again the third day. This news saddened them but they did not comprehend the significance of it and feared to ask for clarification (Mt 17.22-23; Mk 9.30-32; Lk 9.45). Sometimes His friends thought that He had lost His reason and tried to restrain Him (Mk 3.21).When He spoke of the One who had sent Him, they did not understand that He was referring to His Father (Jn 8.27). Christ also taught in parables to reveal truth to those who sought it. Even then, the disciples did not always understand the parables (Jn 10.6). His triumphal entry into Jerusalem had been predicted in Scripture, but once again we read, "These things understood not his disciples at the first: but when Jesus was glorified, then remembered they that these things were written of him, and that they had done these things unto him" (Jn 12.16).

When it came to the provision of daily needs, including bread for a multitude, the Saviour had to say, "O ye of little faith" (Mt 6.30; 16.8) When the disciples were concerned about their personal protection in a storm, He said, "Why are ye fearful, O ye of little faith? Then he arose, and rebuked the winds and the sea; and there was a great calm" (Mt 8.26). To Peter came the words, "O thou of little faith, wherefore didst thou doubt?" (Mt 14.31). They were His inner circle of friends and yet they failed Him often.

Misrepresented

The Lord had to bear many false accusations from His detractors. They feared Him, but that did not stop them insulting Him: "Behold a man gluttonous, and a winebibber, a friend of publicans and sinners" (Mt 11.19). Several times over, John tells us that Christ's presence caused a division amongst the people (Jn 7.43; 9.16; 10.19). The Pharisees were quick to proclaim, "This man is not of God, because he kept not the Sabbath day" (Jn 9.16). When Christ spoke of His power to lay down His life and take it again, having receive this authority from His Father, some said, "He hath a devil, and is mad" (Jn 10.20). A more serious accusation was that He performed His miracles in the power of Beelzebub, the prince of demons (Mt 12.24; Mk 3.22; Lk 11.15).

The Pharisees had no doubts that the Lord Jesus Christ was claiming to be divine; however, they refused to believe His claim and labelled it blasphemy. Because they did not have the authority to try capital offences and pronounce the death sentence, they had to frame a case against Him that would catch the attention of their Roman rulers: "And they began to accuse him, saying, We found this fellow perverting the nation, and forbidding to give tribute to Caesar, saying that he himself is Christ a King" (Lk 23.2). Pilate, the Roman governor, was conscious of his own responsibilities to put down any subversion or treasonous activity, and so he was quickly involved.

Then there was the matter of their corruption. Christ's opponents sought to find false witnesses but their task proved more difficult than they had thought at first. The quality of the fabricated testimony was so poor that even the lies did not agree. At last, two witnesses were enlisted to say the same thing (Mt 26.59-61). After Christ's resurrection, despite the efforts of the authorities to seal and guard the tomb, His enemies scrambled to discount the truth that confronted them. They resorted to bribery: "And when they were assembled with the elders, and had taken counsel, they gave large money unto the soldiers, Saying, Say ye, His disciples came by night, and stole him away while we slept" (Mt 28.12-13).

Mistreated

Hatred against the Lord Jesus arose early on in His ministry, and soon His enemies were plotting to destroy Him (Mk 3.6). On a number of occasions they tried to kill Him but He passed through their midst. In Nazareth they were furious when He spoke of Gentiles who had received the blessing of God instead of the Jews. Their anger flared up and they "thrust him out of the city, and led him unto the brow of the hill whereon their city was built, that they might cast him down headlong. But he passing through the midst of them went his way" (Lk 4.29-30). On another occasion "took they up stones to cast at him: but Jesus hid himself, and went out of the temple, going through the midst of them, and so passed by" (Jn 8.59). Few details are given; only that He evaded them. His time had not yet come (Jn 7.30).

The illegal mock trial was preceded by Judas' betrayal and the arrest of Christ in the garden. The mob came heavily armed and binding Him, they led Him away. Rough hands, coarse words, mockery and scorn, shame and spitting, the scourge, the thorns, the nails – He bore them all. They hated Him without a cause (Jn 15.25). He had already warned His disciples that because the world hated Him, they should expect to be hated too (Jn 15.18).

Rejected

He came to His own people in mercy and grace and yet they would not receive Him (Jn 1.11). He had presented Himself to them as their King. He had loved them and sought to bless them. By many wonderful works He had shown them that He was the promised Messiah, but they would have none of it (Jn 19.15). They were looking for a national liberator who would overthrow their Roman rulers and bring them political liberty and material prosperity. They were not interested in being confronted by their sins and told of their need of salvation.

The religious leaders had worked hard behind the scenes, stirring up the mob with wild and false accusations. They feared Christ's popularity with the common people and they were determined to put an end to it; their own position and influence was at stake. Pilate was well aware of their motives (Mt 27.18). The common people who welcomed Christ into Jerusalem would a few days later be calling for His death; their impassioned cries revealed the verdict of their hearts: "Away with this man, and release unto us Barabbas"; "Away with him, away with him, crucify him…We have no king but Caesar" (Jn 18.40; 19.15).

In all of these trials and sufferings at the hands of men, Christ could see the end from the beginning: "who for the joy that was set before him endured the cross, despising the shame" (Heb 12.2). His perspective went far beyond this earth. He knew that He would soon be returning in glory to the Father but that His message of life and hope would be carried to every corner of the world, bringing salvation to millions. He was fully aware that a day would come when He would return to earth in glory and majesty (Mt 16.27; 24.30; 25.31). He would be fully vindicated and universally acknowledged as the King of kings and Lord of lords (Phil 2.9-11; 1Tim 6.15). Today, we too can rejoice that all of His sufferings are over and the once crucified Christ is now the exalted and glorified Christ at the right hand of the throne of God in heaven.

A PERSONAL REMINDER
To become more like Christ, I must:
- overcome temptation by relying upon God's Word
- be prepared to suffer for Him
- remember there is joy ahead.

CHAPTER 8

His Gracious Words

Moving from the inner and private aspects of Christ's life to the more public features of His ministry upon earth, we now consider the things He said. Words have great power, either for good or ill. In the person of the Lord Jesus Christ, God spoke to men (Heb 1.2). Christ was the incarnate Word, the audible as well as visible expression of God living amongst men. Think for a moment of some of the words He spoke and the variety of needs they met:

1. Simple words of invitation: "Come unto me" (Mt 11.28)
2. Saving words of life: "Believe me" (Jn 14.11)
3. Soothing words of comfort: "Weep not" (Lk 7.13)
4. Stirring words of hope: "I will come again" (Jn 14.3)
5. Sovereign words of command: "Peace, be still" (Mk 4.39)
6. Strong words of rebuke: "Get thee behind me, Satan" (Lk 4.8)
7. Solemn words of warning: "Except ye repent, ye shall all likewise perish" (Lk 13.3)
8. Stern words of judgment: "Woe unto you" (Mt 23.14).

In the way He spoke, Christ was so different from us: He never hesitated before speaking because of indecision; He never pulled up in mid-sentence because of doubt; He never had a lingering regret after speaking. There were no confessions, no apologies, and no retractions. He said the right thing at the right time to the right person because He knew the particular need of each. He had time for individuals as well as the crowds. He meant every word He said and those to whom He was speaking had His undivided attention. Every word glorified the Father, and at the end of His earthly ministry He could confidently say to His Father, "I have given them thy word…thy word is truth" (Jn 17.14, 17).

When He spoke, people responded in different ways. Some received His words of life and were blessed. The woman of Samaria (Jn 4) had a wonderful conversation with Christ as He rested at the side of Jacob's well. At first she was surprised to find a Jew who spoke kindly to her, but then she went on to discover that He was also a prophet who knew everything about her. Finally, she was to learn that He was the promised Messiah, the Christ, whom she could believe in. Her joyful testimony was of the One who "told me all things that ever I did" (v 29).

Others rejected Christ's words and opposed Him. His enemies tried to catch Him out in His speech and then ultimately to silence Him by putting Him to death (Mk 12.13). Luke tells us that a number of them were sent to find fault with Christ but "they could not take hold of his words before the people: and they marvelled at his answer, and held their peace" (Lk 20.20, 26). John tells us of the officers who were commandeered by the Pharisees and chief priests to go and arrest the Saviour. Instead of accomplishing this, they could only listen and marvel at His wonderful words. When they returned to their masters and were asked to explain why they were empty-handed, all they could say was, "Never man spake like this man" (Jn 7.46).

The Lord Jesus Christ was inseparably one with His message, speaking of "me, and my words" (Jn 15.7). To believe His words was to accept Him: "Whosoever therefore shall be ashamed of me and of my words in this adulterous and sinful generation; of him also shall the Son of man be ashamed, when he cometh in the glory of his Father with the holy angels" (Mk 8.38; Lk 9.26). Sometimes our personal character has an adverse effect on what we are trying to say because there is a glaring disparity between what we claim to be and what we are seen to be. As a result, our words sound empty and unconvincing. This was never the case with the sinless Son of God.

The Lord spoke with authority

A wonderful illustration of the power of the words of Christ is found in the raising of Lazarus (Jn 11). It is recorded that Jesus spoke three times and each time He issued a short command: "Lazarus, come forth", and there was life; "Roll back the stone", and there was light; "Loose him, and let him go", and there was liberty. By His words alone He raised the dead man. It was no wonder that many of the Jews believed on Him (v 45). On many other occasions He gave simple direct commands that were immediately obeyed.

His words never missed their mark: minds were enlightened; consciences were troubled; hearts were touched. When sinners heard Him speak and were convicted of their sins, they were left with a clear choice: believe Him and be forgiven; refuse Him and be condemned. His words were confrontational and challenging but their ultimate purpose was to bring blessing to needy souls.

The scribes were always referring to scholars from the past to back up their views. The Lord Jesus quoted Scripture, but did not need the words of any other man to support what He was saying. His hearers were astonished because "he taught them as one having authority, and not as the scribes" (Mt 7.29; Mk 1.22). Many of the pronouncements and voluminous writings of the scribes have long been forgotten whereas the words of Christ live on; they are eternal. He could declare, "Heaven and earth shall pass away, but my words shall not pass away" (Mt 24.35).

He spoke simply

Christ illustrated His teaching with word pictures and parables, often referring to the common things of everyday life. Those who lived and worked on the land would listen intently when He spoke of sowing seed or searching for lost sheep. Urban dwellers would look at one another and nod when He spoke of building a house or paying off debts. Married couples might have smiled knowingly when He mentioned wedding feasts. Parents would empathize immediately with the story of a wayward son. Children would enjoy the hide-and-seek tale of a lost coin. Of course, the Saviour's purpose was not to entertain but rather to convict hearts and consciences. The scribes and Pharisees would frown and recoil when He spoke of tombs painted white outside, but full of bones and corruption inside. In His frequent use of parables, the Lord revealed truth to those who sincerely sought it. They were never left in any doubt as to what He meant.

The Saviour also used parables to conceal truth from some of His hearers (Mt 13.10-17); however, the stories themselves were perfectly intelligible to those who earnestly sought after Him. The concealment of truth from His enemies was a result of their unbelief, not the cause of it. They had already rejected Him in their hearts.

He instructed patiently

The disciples, like us, were slow to learn and dull in grasping spiritual truth; they could forget important things they should have remembered. There were gentle rebukes from the Saviour, but He kept on teaching them. As to His method, He often dropped a few lines here and a few lines there on a particular subject. We have already seen that His teaching concerning the Comforter, the Holy Spirit, was expertly woven throughout the ministry of the upper room as recorded by John.

At least three times over He told them of His imminent suffering and death, burial and resurrection. Firstly, He spoke to them in the northern region of Caesarea Philippi where Peter foolishly rebuked Him (Mk 8.27-31). Then He repeated the same in Galilee; still they did not understand (Mk 9.30-32). Finally, moving further south to Jerusalem, He said to the fearful group of disciples, "Behold, we go up to Jerusalem; and the Son of man shall be delivered unto the chief priests, and unto the scribes; and they shall condemn him to death, and shall deliver him to the Gentiles" (Mk 10.32-34). Surely, one might think, by that time they must have grasped the significance of His words? It seems not; they were more interested in their own position in a coming kingdom!

After the resurrection there was a noticeable change in the comprehension of the disciples. They recalled things He had told them before, even as the events were enacted and fulfilled before their eyes (Lk 24.8); "These things understood not his disciples at the first: but when Jesus was glorified, then remembered they that these things were written of him, and that they had done these things unto him" (Jn 12.16).

He spoke graciously

In the synagogue in Nazareth, He read a passage from the scroll of Isaiah (61.1). This foretold the liberating and life-changing ministry of God's perfect Servant. What must have stunned His audience was His declaration that the same Scripture was that day being fulfilled before them: "All bare him witness, and wondered at the gracious words which proceeded out of his mouth. And they said, Is not this Joseph's son?" (Lk 4.22).

Christ was gentle with repentant sinners. One day His detractors hauled before Him a woman whom they had caught in the act of adultery (Jn 8). They reminded Him that the law of Moses prescribed that she should be stoned. Somehow the guilty man had been overlooked. They had no concern at all for the woman but were only using her as a pawn to provoke the Saviour. He stooped down to write on the ground with His finger. When they persisted with their question, He looked up and challenged them, "He that is without sin among you, let him first cast a stone at her." Then, in the moments of silence, as He stooped down to write again on the dust of the ground, they made their exit one by one, filing out in their shame until only the woman and the Saviour remained. Not one stone had been cast. How must the woman have felt when, fully aware of her guilt and the punishment the law demanded, she heard Him say to her, "Neither do I condemn thee: go and sin no more" (v 11)? He did not condone her sin but forgave it, and urged her to completely forsake it.

The words the Saviour uttered from the cross are beyond our comprehension; they display a measure of grace that confounds us. First of all, there was a prayer for His tormentors: "Father, forgive them; for they know not what they do" (Lk 23.34); then there was a word for the dying thief: "To day shalt thou be with me in paradise"(Lk 23.43). He also spoke to Mary, His mother, and John, the disciple whom He loved: "Woman, behold thy son!" and, addressing John, "Behold thy mother!" (Jn 19.26-27). His concern was for their mutual blessing and care. He thought of others first.

He spoke faithfully
The Lord Jesus spoke only truth. He acknowledged that His Father's word was the truth and He was communicating and revealing it to men. Such truth was unchanging in character and eternal in duration (Mk 13.31; Lk 21.33).

Sometimes the Lord Jesus asked questions. Ninety or so of these are recorded in the Gospels. He never did this to learn something He did not know, but rather to challenge the hearts of men and women. On occasions He had to correct His hearers' misconceptions: "Do ye not perceive, that whatsoever thing from without entereth into the man, it cannot defile him …?" (Mk 7.18). His questions also challenged their faith: once after a storm He asked His disciples, "Why are ye fearful, O ye of little faith?" (Mt 8.26); and of two blind men He asked, "Believe ye that I am able to do this?" to which they answered, "Yea, Lord" (Mt 9.28). He drew forth a confession of faith one day when He asked a strange question in the midst of a milling and jostling crowd, "Who touched me?" (Lk 8.45). The woman who had just touched the hem of His garment and had been healed, came out into the open by publicly confessing that she was the one who had come seeking His help.

When He was confronted by those who were seeking to oppose Him, He was able immediately to read their hearts. All of their questions were insincere and loaded with barbs; they were constantly probing and seeking to find fault in order to condemn Him. When the Lord responded to their questions by asking another question, He was not trying to be evasive. Rather, He was seeking to convict them in their hearts. Often they could not answer Him, and so the encounter would come to an abrupt end.

The silences of the Saviour were as eloquent as His words. He spoke no words of self-defence at His trial. When the truth was spoken, He concurred, but when He was falsely accused, He said nothing. The high priest tried to provoke Him into responding to the false testimonies, but "Jesus held his peace" (Mt 26.63), and before Pilate too, "Jesus gave him no answer" (Jn 19.9). Herod questioned Him with many words but "he answered him nothing" (Lk 23.9).

What about us?
We learn much from the example of the Saviour in His speech. James reminds us of the great power and influence of the tongue (Jas 3.2-12). Our speech can bring great blessing when it is consecrated to the Master and used for His glory. On the other hand, although the tongue is only "a little member", it can cause great harm. Nuclear power has been employed in many beneficial ways but that same power has been used in other harmful ways to completely destroy thousands of lives – just like the misuse of the tongue.

How easy it is to become careless in our speech and to be drawn into malicious gossip. Many of us have witnessed how quickly the tone of a conversation has changed for the worse, even amongst Christians. What was intended to be an evening of spiritual fellowship got off to a promising enough start, but there came a turning point when a jarring note of harsh criticism was introduced; by the end of the evening, someone else (in their absence) had fallen victim to a character assassination. The speakers had forgotten the truth of the words that used to be displayed in many homes: "Christ is the Head of this house; the Unseen Guest at every meal; the Silent Listener to every conversation." Were we to realize the reality of His presence, we would surely speak differently.

It is not as if the Scriptures leave us in any doubt as to the dangers of evil speaking: "Speak not evil one of another, brethren. He that speaketh evil of his brother, and judgeth his brother, speaketh evil of the law, and judgeth the law: but if thou judge the law, thou art not a doer of the law, but a judge" (Jas 4.11); "But if ye bite and devour one another, take heed that ye be not consumed one of another" (Gal 5.15).

The Lord Jesus never trafficked in innuendoes. He told it just as it was. He commended those in whom He perceived a sincerity of heart, and yet He did not flatter; He condemned others who were only hypocrites. He warned the disciples in private about "the leaven of the Pharisees" but He addressed the offenders directly in public. He did not say anything behind their backs that He would not say to their faces. His righteous indignation was in response to their evil and perverted character. Nothing had missed His notice; even their thoughts were known to Him. When we speak of others, we might ask ourselves three questions: Is it true? Is it necessary? Is it glorifying to the Lord?

Many of us also fail when it comes to speaking of spiritual things, especially of our Saviour Himself. We wax eloquent on more mundane topics – the weather, politics, or the economy – but we suddenly become embarrassed and tongue-tied when the subject changes to something spiritual. We recall the first flush of newborn faith when the words just tumbled out and we could scarcely be silenced as we testified of the goodness of our Saviour. Then, as time passed, our zeal waned and we became reluctant witnesses who would more often prefer to remain mute. Perhaps we all need to cultivate afresh this discipline of learning to testify of the great things that He has done for us, and to be ready to give a reason of the hope that it is in us (1 Pet 3.15). One of the hardest places to witness is in one's own home but we recall that the Lord Jesus told the Gadarenian man, "Go home to thy friends, and tell them how great things the Lord hath done for thee, and hath had compassion on thee" (Mk 5.19).

In the service of the Lord, simple direct speech is a necessity. We should rightly be ashamed of ourselves if we as listeners cannot follow a preacher's message because of our spiritual dullness, but the preacher or teacher also has a responsibility to make the message easily understood. There is no virtue at all in 'being deep', as it is sometimes put, and leaving the audience wondering what it was all about.

The control of the tongue is a rare discipline and a sign of Christian maturity (Jas 3.2). The psalmist prayed for the Lord's help in this: "Set a watch, O Lord, before my mouth; keep the door of my lips" (Ps 141.3). May our speech "be alway with grace, seasoned with salt" (Col 4.6).

A PERSONAL REMINDER
To become more like Christ, I must:
- speak with grace and love
- focus on what is true and profitable
- testify often of God's goodness and great salvation.

CHAPTER 9

His Mighty Works

When we think of the works of the Lord Jesus Christ during His time upon earth, we tend to focus on His miracles: these demonstrated His divine power and greatness. Many of them were carried out simply at His command. Just as in creation, He only had to speak and it was done.

Christ could rebuke the tempest and say to the stormy waters, "Peace, be still", and immediately there was a great calm (Mk 4.39). After a night toiling on the sea, Peter confessed to the Lord that they had caught nothing but when the Lord told him to launch out into the deep, Peter replied, "at thy word I will let down the net" (Lk 5.5). The result was that they caught so many fish that the net broke and the boats were in danger of sinking.

On two occasions Christ fed thousands of hungry people using what seemed to be meagre resources. At a wedding in Cana of Galilee, He turned water into the best wine. These things were always done for the benefit and blessing of others; however, when He hungered in the wilderness, He refused to make even one stone into bread. When He hung upon the cross and cried, "I thirst", He did not use His divine power to meet His own physical need.

He was able to heal many different conditions: blindness, deafness, paralysis, leprosy, fever, oedema, anaemia and convulsions. All of these were serious and debilitating but the Lord healed them immediately and completely, in stark contrast to the professed 'faith healing' services of today. There were three sick people whom He healed from a distance: a centurion's servant, a Gentile woman's daughter and a nobleman's son. As we have already noted, there were three people that He raised from the dead.

In everything He did, Christ sought to glorify God and bring blessing to others. Nothing was done out of self-interest. His life was not divided into the sacred and the secular. All of His service was carried out with a sacrificial spirit. It was never a question of worship or service; it was always both. What was done for God was also for man: what was done for man was also for God. There was nothing mundane or unimportant to Him in His daily activities, and individuals were not neglected in favour of the clamouring crowds.

He was busy
The Lord Jesus was always busy in service. He was often mobbed and thronged by people who had great expectations that He would bless them in their need. He was aware of their different motives: some hoped for a free meal and others wanted to be entertained by a spectacle. There were those too who sought to find fault with Him, but all who looked to Him in genuine faith were never disappointed.

At the opening of Mark's Gospel we read of one such busy day in His life. He had an early start, beginning with the Word of God and the teaching of the Scriptures. That day, in the synagogue in Capernaum, there was a man with an unclean spirit; the Lord healed him. As soon as He left the synagogue, He entered into the house of Simon and Andrew for a bedside consultation, healing Simon's mother-in-law who was afflicted with a great fever. One would have thought that at the end of the day He should have enjoyed a well earned rest. It was not to be. After the sun had set, "all the city" gathered outside the door and He healed many more during a late-evening surgery. "Well," we might say, "He could lie in the next morning." Again,

He surprises and delights us: "Rising up a great while before the day, he went out, and departed into a solitary place, and there prayed" (Mk 1.35). He had an early-morning appointment that He must keep; His communion with the Father could not be neglected or even postponed.

It is likely that most of the journeys Christ made were on foot, and at that pace He had many encounters with different people along the way. The geographical boundaries of His ministry were small and yet today, His fame has spread to every corner of the globe. Wherever He went, He dispensed blessing upon the needy that trusted Him. They welcomed Him into their hearts and homes. Where He was met by unbelief, the blessing was limited. We recall that there was no room for Him in Bethlehem at the time of His birth. There was no room for Him in Nazareth where He had grown up. One day the people of that place, provoked by His teaching, took Him to a steep hill outside the town and would have cast Him over the edge to a premature death. At the end of His life there was no room for Him either in Jerusalem. He was rejected by all of the religious, political and social circles of that time, and crucified outside the city wall.

His diligence in service comes as a rebuke to many of us who are content to cruise along as comfortably and leisurely as possible. We might be good at attending the meetings of the local Christians and even take part in some avenue of service, but we have low levels of tolerance for extra burdens laid upon us. We can envy people of a more dynamic disposition who appear to be in constant motion, tackling life head-on. But they too are often intolerant, particularly if anyone or anything gets in their way; they can be insensitive to the needs of others. We say that the first are "laid back" and the second are "driven". Christ was neither; He was led.

We cannot imagine the Saviour rushing and dashing about in a flurry of dust and frenzied activity. Always under the control and guidance of the Holy Spirit, He moved in a dignified way. At times He was misjudged and accused of having delayed in responding to an urgent need. That was the case when He arrived at Bethany after Lazarus had died. Mary told Him that if He had come straight away when first informed, Lazarus would have lived; however, there was divine purpose in it all. By the end of the story a greater glory was revealed.

He was available

We struggle when we are unexpectedly interrupted in the middle of our work. What we regard as interruptions are often, in fact, special opportunities sent to us by God. When Christ was on the way to see Jairus's daughter (Mk 5), there was one such interruption and apparent delay. A poor woman, weak because of disease, came trembling behind Him to touch the hem of His garment in the hope of being healed. He stopped to address her and encourage her to publicly confess her faith. As she told Him "all the truth" (v 33), giving her long medical history and speaking of her many unsuccessful efforts to find a cure, we can imagine that the Saviour gave her His full attention and listened to her every word. Was Jairus growing increasingly anxious and impatient?

Then, the alarming news came to Jairus that it was too late; his little girl had died. Immediately the Saviour comforted and encouraged him: "Be not afraid, only believe" (v 36). When they arrived at the home they were confronted by the insincere wailing of the professional mourners; the Lord sent them away. There was also the scornful laughter of those who doubted His power. These were proved wrong when soon afterwards the young girl appeared, alive and well.

He was focused

Christ knew exactly why He had come to earth. The words of Psalm 40 are fitting: "Then said I, Lo, I come: in the volume of the book it is written of me, I delight to do thy will, O my God:

yea, thy law is within my heart" (vv 7-8). He was willing to leave the glories of heaven and come down to do His Father's will. He had a mission to accomplish, and He set His face steadfastly to go to Jerusalem (Lk 9.51). He would not be diverted from the pathway that led to the cross. He regarded it as a baptism of rejection, suffering and judgment: "I have a baptism to be baptized with; and how am I straitened till it be accomplished!" (Lk 12.50). He came to seek and to save that which was lost, and to give abundant life to those who were dead in their sins. The Father sent Him to be the Saviour of the world, and He became a propitiation for our sins so that we might live through Him (1 Jn 4.9, 10, 14).

Some people have not discovered that God has a specific work for them to do. They expect preachers, teachers of God's Word and missionaries to know, but as for themselves, they have only vague thoughts as to their spiritual vocation. They aim at nothing and usually end up hitting it. God has an individual plan for all our lives and when we learn what that plan is, we should seek to be faithful in fulfilling it by His grace. It may not involve us leaving our homes or our employment; it may not be a public or a prominent ministry; nevertheless, it will require us to give of our best, and keep at it.

He was loving
Our attitude to the young, the weak and underprivileged tells a lot about us. If we court only the company of those whom we regard as being important or those whom we judge might be of use to us, we betray the fact that we are out of touch and out of harmony with the mind of the Master. In general, the mighty and influential did not have much time for Christ, but the Scriptures tell us that it was the common people who heard Him gladly (Mk 12.37).

Little children, regarded by others as being just a nuisance, were welcome in His arms. Lepers, shunned by everyone else, received a healing touch from Him. Tax collectors, used to being despised alongside sinners, found that He would willingly visit their homes. Poor widows, used to being exploited, were blessed and honoured by Him; He took special note of their love and devotion. Prostitutes, accustomed to being abused and mistreated by men, did not shrink back from Him. A hardened criminal, hanging upon a cross and about to die, looked to Him and believed at the eleventh hour; He was promised paradise.

There were those who turned away from Christ but He loved them still. Such was the rich young ruler who came running to the Lord and asked how he might inherit eternal life. He claimed to have kept the commandments, but there was a fierce battle in his heart and the Lord knew it. His riches had the greatest claim upon him; that was the very same matter the Lord challenged when He told him to sell all that he had and give it to the poor. The Scripture says, "Jesus beholding him loved him" (Mk 10.21).

He was gracious
One day a woman, well known to have a sinful past, sought Christ out in the home of Simon, the Pharisee. She had brought an alabaster box of ointment, and weeping, she began to wash His feet with her tears, kissing them, wiping them with her hair and anointing them with the ointment. Simon was taken aback and began to wonder, "If Jesus were a prophet, how could He not know the sort of woman she was? Why did He not prevent her touching Him?" The Lord knew exactly what Simon was thinking and so He told him a story of two debtors who owed vastly different sums of money. Both were unable to pay off their debts but both were freely forgiven. The Lord asked Simon which one of the two debtors would have loved their forgiving creditor the most? Simon rightly answered that it would have been the one who had been forgiven the most. The Lord went on to explain the depth of the woman's love: "Her sins, which are many, are forgiven; for she loved much"; and

He said unto her, "Thy sins are forgiven ... Thy faith hath saved thee; go in peace" (Lk 7.48, 50).

When Christ seemed to deny an initial request, His purpose was to test the sincerity of a person's faith. He would then grant the request and bless abundantly. When a Gentile woman came to Him seeking a cure for her daughter and crying out for mercy, Jesus was silent at first (Mt 15.22-23). This caused the disciples to ask that the woman be sent away. When at last Jesus spoke, His words gave no encouragement; He declared that He had been sent to the house of Israel, not to the Gentiles. The woman did not give up. We read that she worshipped Him, and again pleaded before Him, "Lord, help me" (v 25). Still He held back and spoke of how "the children's bread" (blessings for the Jews) was not meant for "the dogs" (the Gentiles). We must admire the response of this woman: "Truth, Lord: yet even the dogs eat of the crumbs which fall from their master's table" (v 27). In effect, she was imploring Him for just a small crumb of blessing. At last the Lord, who valued her persistence, gave her a commendation that will never be forgotten: "O woman, great is thy faith." Furthermore, her daughter was completely healed from that moment (v 28).

He was personal
People who drew near to Christ were welcomed. Others who had physical difficulty in coming to Him were not disadvantaged; He drew near to them. An attitude of aloofness was never seen in the life of the Lord. Often He came alongside individuals and, with a tender touch, He would take them by the hand. Simon's mother-in-law was just one such needy person. He took her by the hand and lifted her up (Mk 1.31). He did the same with Jairus's daughter, taking her by the hand and commanding her to arise (Mk 5.41). The plight of a young man who was afflicted by severe convulsions was brought to the attention of the Lord Jesus; the Lord healed him and "took him by the hand and lifted him up" (Mk 9.27). He was always giving people a lift! At Bethsaida, He took a blind man by the

hand and, leading him outside the city, He put His hands upon his eyes and healed him.

We have already referred to that incident in John's Gospel where we find Christ resting beside a well. The intense heat and unrelenting glare of the sun had taken their toll, leaving Him weary and thirsty. He had purposely chosen a route not normally travelled by a Jew so that He could meet one individual, a Samaritan woman; she was important to Him. After asking her for a drink of water, a conversation ensued that took an unusual direction: it ended up with the woman believing in Him. We do not know if Christ ever received the drink He requested from her, but we can be sure that she was fully satisfied with the living water that He gave to her that day. Others from the city received eternal life through faith in Him, as well as the woman – their souls would never thirst again (Jn 4.39, 41).

Christian work is always at a risk of being conducted at a distance and becoming impersonal. We can be busy preaching and teaching the Word of God from a platform but avoid direct interaction with ordinary people and their many problems. Crowds can obscure individuals. With our technology we can post off circular letters and batch e-mails to far-flung places all around the world, and yet miss out in that truly personal touch. Today, more and more individuals are getting lost in the middle of societies that treat them merely as numbers. We need to reaffirm the value of each individual soul created in the image of God. He loves every one of them and Christ displayed that love in fullest measure.

The record of Scripture concerning the works of the Lord Jesus is a selective one; it is certain that in heaven we will have much more to learn about the great things He did. John spent over three years with the Lord and later he wrote five books of the New Testament, but even He had to confess that "there are also many other things which Jesus did, the which, if they should be written every one, I suppose that even the world itself could not contain the books that should be written. Amen" (Jn 21.25).

A PERSONAL REMINDER
To become more like Christ, I must:
- seek to follow God's plan for my life
- work for Him with all my strength
- show His love to others.

CHAPTER 10

His Love for Family, Friends and Foes

If we were asked to choose one word to sum up the life of Christ, we might well decide on the word 'others': He came to live, and to die for the blessing of others. As we briefly review His interactions with different people, we again face a particular challenge in trying to write about Christ. It is this – the complementary themes of His holiness and truth, His love and grace, keep reoccurring. They are unavoidable. We have already thought of these themes when considering other aspects of His life; it is just the same when we think of His relationship to other people. His holiness and truth meant that when He saw others, the veneer was stripped away, their sins and failings were fully exposed, and they were made to face up to the reality of their condition before God. But when we add to these Christ's love and grace, we find that He accepted people just as they were. When they confessed what they were, guilty sinners, and recognized who He was, the only Saviour, they received great blessing. It is still the same today: there is nobody that He does not love – needy sinners are always welcome. We will focus on just three groups: His family, His friends and His foes.

His love for His family

Jesus spent almost thirty years of His life in Nazareth as part of a humble family. We recall that in their poverty Mary and Joseph had only been able to bring two small birds for an offering when they went up to Jerusalem, shortly after the birth of Jesus (Lk 2.24). Joseph was a carpenter by trade and well known in his home town. Every Jewish boy was expected to learn a trade; it is likely that Jesus served His apprenticeship in the family business. Carpentry was an honest way to earn a living and support one's family, but carpenters were not generally regarded as being highly educated. Nazareth was certainly not the centre for the intelligentsia of the day. That was the reason for the people's surprise when they heard Christ teach in the local synagogue: "Whence hath this man this wisdom, and these mighty works? Is not this the carpenter's son? is not his mother called Mary? and his brethren, James, and Joses, and Simon, and Judas? And his sisters, are they not all with us? Whence then hath this man all these things?" (Mt 13.54-56). Unfortunately, their prejudice prevented them from believing in Him; consequently, Christ's ministry was constrained in that locality.

From the verses above we learn that Jesus was the eldest in a family of at least seven children. Joseph is only mentioned at the beginning of Christ's earthly life; it is possible that he died some time before Christ left home at the age of thirty. As the eldest son, He would then have been chiefly responsible for the upkeep of the family. In Mark's account of the same story, Christ Himself is called "the carpenter, the son of Mary" (Mk 6.3).

The family is at the centre of God's plan for a stable society. Today there are all sorts of godless philosophies swirling around which would undermine the whole fabric of the family unit. Some activists are campaigning vigorously to redefine the structure and function of family life. Listening to their calls for change, one could almost conclude that the whole concept of a father and mother caring for their children and bringing them up in the fear of the Lord must be outdated and inadequate to meet today's challenges. The truth is that the abandoning of these principles of God's Word is leaving behind a mounting trail of emotional debris and human tragedy in many societies the world over.

Some of us have had a secure and sheltered upbringing in a Christian home. Others have had to struggle in much less favourable domestic circumstances. But surely we can all take heart when we remember that the Son of God grew up in a large working class family in which He had many responsibilities and burdens. What would have added to the difficulty of His situation was that He was largely misunderstood. His parents misjudged Him when they mistakenly left Him behind after a visit to Jerusalem. We read that many years later His brothers (really half-brothers) did not believe in Him (Jn 7.3-5). They thought that He was merely on a quest for fame, and therefore they urged Him go to Judaea where He would have a wider audience. It is only when we come to the book of Acts that we discover His brothers had come to personal faith in Him and were meeting to pray with the other believers in Jerusalem (Acts 1.14). James went on to write one of the books of the New Testament that goes by his name; it is possible too that Judas (or Jude), another of the Lord's brothers, was the author of the short penultimate book of the New Testament.

There is a touching scene at the cross when the Lord Jesus in His agony looked down at His mother standing with the other faithful women. She was accompanied by the disciple John. He spoke first to His mother: "Woman, behold thy son!"; then He addressed John: "Behold thy mother!" (Jn 19.26-27). By these special commands Christ was making arrangements for the care of Mary after His death. In the midst of His own suffering there was loving concern for the welfare of His mother. He was fully committed to His family from beginning to end.

We are all learners when it comes to family life; we never know what new challenges or difficulties lie just around the corner. The needs of our families go far beyond us providing for them materially; there are deep emotional needs that are sometimes overlooked. Family members need time for one another and Christian homes should be full of love, warmth and the reality of a daily walk with God. Children will be the first to notice if their parents act in one way in public, but behave in a completely different way at home. The most important needs of all are spiritual ones; Christian parents long for the salvation and spiritual development of their children. Indeed, much grace and wisdom is needed in preparing young minds and hearts to live for God in a godless world.

His love for His friends

The Lord Jesus valued friendship. He appreciated the kindness and hospitality of the family of Lazarus, Mary and Martha. When He was in their home, they lavished love upon Him and He loved them. Mary represents the worshipper, Martha the worker, and Lazarus the witness to the power of Christ. Mary's custom was to be at His feet, learning from Him, but she also honoured Him by anointing His feet with ointment and wiping them with her hair (Jn 11.2).

On one occasion Martha was busy as usual preparing and serving their special guest, but Mary sat at the Lord's feet, enjoying fellowship with Him. Martha complained at being left alone to serve; she had to be gently rebuked. It was not Martha's work that was wrong – someone had to cook, serve and do the washing-up – but it was her resentful attitude that was at fault. Her sister, Mary, was not slacking or trying to avoid the work; she was only making the best use of the opportunity to listen to the Lord. It is possible that after the Lord had departed, she was as busy in the kitchen as Martha. Despite that moment of domestic tension, Bethany provided a welcome haven for the Lord. Not far away from the village, His enemies were conniving and plotting against Him in the city of Jerusalem (Jn 11.18; Mt 21.17).

The friendship was not all one way. The record of Scripture reveals that in their hour of crisis, with the sickness and death of Lazarus, the Lord Jesus showed that He was there to support them, just as they had supported Him. When He wept at the grave of Lazarus, the Jews exclaimed, "Behold, how he loved him!" (Jn 11.36).

There is no record in Scripture that the Lord ever slept a night in Jerusalem. Perhaps He was never made welcome there. Despite the city being the centre of the religious world, He found much that troubled Him there. The temple service had become corrupt and on two occasions we find Him cleansing the precincts (Jn 2.13-17; Mt 21.12-13); it had become nothing more than a marketplace full of dubious characters and dishonest dealers. The whole nation of Israel had become spiritually barren; there was nothing fruitful for God. They were just like a fig tree that had plenty of foliage, giving a promise of fruit, but in the end bearing none. They were busy with religion but had little place in their hearts for God or His Son.

The Lord spent over three years in the close company of twelve men who were hand-picked after a whole night spent in prayer. They were a motley group from different backgrounds. As we know, one of them was an impostor, Judas Iscariot, and all along he acted the part and deceived everyone except the Lord Jesus. The choice of Judas was not a mistake; it was an act of supreme grace in fulfilment of God's will. He would eventually betray the Lord and yet find no satisfaction in the pieces of silver He had bargained for. In a fit of depression, He took his own life and died in his sins.

One thing that strikes us about the Lord is that He was so patient with these men. They were just like us, being slow to learn and quick to forget; with their stumbling steps and bumbling words they made the same mistakes time and again. And yet Christ did not write them off. He kept on loving them and teaching them, gently rebuking them when they erred and frequently reminding them when they forgot. His constant labour of love was evidence of His total commitment to His friends as well as to His family. In the end, after His resurrection, these same men carried on the work of the ascended Christ, and the success of their labours has resulted in untold blessing to millions of souls in every corner of the globe.

Although He knew their faults, Christ took these men into His confidence and revealed His purposes to them. He told them of the great events that lay ahead for Him in the plan of God: He would be betrayed, rejected and crucified, and after three days He would rise again. There was an openness and directness about His words: He must have been often disappointed at their dullness and unfaithfulness but He did not hold back in any way from reaching out to them. He was soon going to prove the depth of His love by laying down His life for them: "Greater love hath no man than this, that a man lay down his life for his friends. Ye are my friends, if ye do whatsoever I command you. Henceforth I call you not servants; for the servant knoweth not what his lord doeth: but I have called you friends; for all things that I have heard of my Father I have made known unto you" (Jn 15.13-15).

We cannot be close friends to everyone. The example of the Lord would show us that He had an inner circle of friends (Peter, James and John) amongst the twelve disciples. There were others also outside the twelve who were personally commissioned by Him. On one occasion He appointed a large group of seventy to do His work and challenged them with these words: "The harvest truly is great, but the labourers are few: pray ye therefore the Lord of the harvest, that he would send forth labourers into his harvest" (Lk 10.2). He sent them out in pairs, recognizing the importance of people pulling together in the work of God.

There were personal moments with individuals, and often a specific word for a particular need. What must Peter have thought when the Lord said to him, "Simon, Simon, behold, Satan hath desired to have you, that he may sift you as wheat: But I have prayed for thee, that thy faith fail not: and when thou art converted, strengthen thy brethren" (Lk 22.31-32)? Peter must have been sobered to hear of the severe trial that lay ahead; however, he would have been comforted to know that Christ was praying specifically for him. Christ was loyal to these, His friends; He never gossiped about them or criticized them behind their backs. He was a friend who stuck closer than a brother.

His love for His enemies

There is a great difference between the Old and the New Testaments regarding a person's attitude to enemies. For example, in the Old Testament we read a number of psalms written by King David in which he called upon God to destroy those who were against him. The language is often forceful and vengeful, in keeping with the principle of "an eye for an eye, and a tooth for a tooth" (Ex 21.24; Mt 5.38). At the same time, these writings should be balanced by recalling David's actions when he had several opportunities to slay King Saul, his persistent enemy, but instead he held back and spared his life: "The Lord forbid that I should stretch forth my hand against the Lord's anointed" (1 Sam 26.11). Saul had not been so reticent about trying to pin David to the wall with a spear, but God preserved the future king, a man after His own heart.

The Lord taught that we should love our enemies: "Ye have heard that it hath been said, Thou shalt love thy neighbour, and hate thine enemy. But I say unto you, Love your enemies, bless them that curse you, do good to them that hate you, and pray for them which despitefully use you, and persecute you" (Mt 5.43-44). When Peter drew his sword to strike one of those who came to arrest the Lord in the garden, Christ commanded him, "Put up again thy sword into his place: for all they that take the sword shall perish with the sword" (Mt 26.52). The Lord had legions of angels at His command but He left them unbidden.

There is a general viewpoint in the world that Christian pacifism is nothing more than cowardice mixed with dreamy idealism. The argument, briefly stated, proceeds like this: to love enemies is really to indulge them; by so doing, one encourages them to take advantage of others and be even more cruel; such appeasement breeds tyranny. All of these views hold good if we consider nothing else above or beyond this world; however, from a perspective that takes into account heavenly values and future realities, the situation is markedly different. If I have sought to love my enemies with a Christlike love and they do not respond positively to it, they will stand condemned by that same love in a coming day of judgment. They will have no excuse, and I will be clear of responsibility for their plight. God will avenge His own in that day and recompense fully those that suffered wrongfully.

It takes real strength of character to love those who wrong you. The easy thing and the natural thing is to try to strike back according to the philosophy, "Don't get mad; get even." Christ chose a different path; in His hours of suffering upon the cross, He prayed for those who hated Him, "Father, forgive them; for they know not what they do" (Lk 23.34). He had fearlessly challenged them and denounced their hypocrisy; He had been angered by their wicked abuse of others and pronounced woe upon them. Not once did He excuse their evil, but still He loved them.

Although we will never be treated as He was, in the experiences of life we do come across those who dislike us and oppose us. Even amongst Christians there are sometimes bitter divisions perpetuated by old grudges and strong feelings of animosity. Our reaction to these many challenges reveals just how much progress we have really made in the quest of becoming more like Christ.

> Are we adept at a stinging reply for every imagined insult, or have we learnt the power of silence?
> Are we masters at plotting revenge, or do we bring the burden before the Lord and let it go?
> Do we want to see every wrong we have suffered put

right now, or are we prepared to let God vindicate us
in His own time?
Can we love and pray for our enemies as He did?

Despite every natural instinct that would stir us up to act in
our own defence, we should remember that love will always
win and gain the ultimate victory in the end.

A PERSONAL REMINDER
To become more like Christ, I must:
- devote time to my family
- be a faithful friend to others
- love and pray for my enemies.

CHAPTER 11

His Death for the World

The death of Christ on the cross of Calvary was the greatest event this world has ever witnessed. Many people that day would have regarded His crucifixion as nothing more than another common execution at the hands of the Roman authorities. Some would have known that Jewish intrigue and local politics were behind it all. Such things had happened before and would soon be forgotten.

What most did not know was that the death of Christ had always been at the centre of God's plan for this world. It became the dividing line in human history but, on a more personal level, it would also become the crucial deciding factor as to one's eternal destiny. Those who believed on the Christ who died would be saved, and those who rejected Him would be lost for ever (Jn 3.36).

Calvary was the fullest expression of divine holiness and divine love. God moved in judgment against sin and at the same time provided salvation for all, so that He could remain just and still be able to justify sinners (Rom 3.26). The love of God was expressed by the giving of His Son for this world (Jn 3.16); Christ came down, leaving behind the glory of heaven, and for over thirty years He lived amongst mankind. His purpose in coming, however, was not to live but to die as a sacrifice upon the cross (I Jn 4.14)). He, the Son of God, became the Sin-bearer for a lost world and the Saviour of every individual who would come to Him in faith. The declaration of these truths remains at the heart of the gospel message and to fail to preach Christ and Him crucified is to miss the mark (1 Cor 1.23; 2.2).

What was also on open display that day was the gross evil of the human heart. The Gospel writers described how Christ was treated at the hands of men. They recorded the events in vivid detail, using a list of verbs that make us shudder: He was taken, bound and led away to be accused and scourged; He was spat upon, buffeted and smitten; then stripped, blindfolded and mocked. He was reviled, derided and railed upon. Finally, He was crucified: the scourge, the thorns and the nails – He bore them all. It was love and nothing else that kept Him there upon the cross.

There was no justice that shameful day: the hateful rulers, lying witnesses, spineless judge, cruel soldiers and hysterical crowd had but one verdict: "Away with him, away with him, crucify him" (Jn 19.15). There was little comfort or support from His disciples – most had fled (Mk 14.50). Thank God, there were faithful women who remained standing beside the cross (Jn 19.25). But when the darkness fell, He was completely alone and forsaken. The sword of divine justice fell with full force upon Him when God laid upon Him the iniquity of us all (Isa 53.6).

So much has been written on this inexhaustible theme that in a few pages we can only focus on several lessons that might help us in our goal of becoming more like Christ. We will think of His death in four ways and also consider the implications of these truths for our own lives.

He offered up His life

"How much more shall the blood of Christ, who through the eternal Spirit offered himself without spot to God, purge your conscience from dead works to serve the living God?" (Heb 9.14).
"For it is not possible that the blood of bulls and of goats should take away sins. Wherefore when he cometh into the world, he saith, Sacrifice

and offering thou wouldest not, but a body hast thou prepared me: In burnt offerings and sacrifices for sin thou hast had no pleasure. Then said I, Lo, I come (in the volume of the book it is written of me,) to do thy will, O God … By the which will we are sanctified through the offering of the body of Jesus Christ once for all" (Heb 10.4-7, 10).

The writer to the Hebrews contrasted the deficiency of the sacrifices that were offered repeatedly upon Jewish altars with the sufficiency of the "once for all" sacrifice of Christ. In the verses above the emphasis is upon a spotless sacrifice that was offered up to God, fulfilling His will and satisfying His righteous judgment against sin. We see too one of those wonderful references to the Trinity: the three persons of the Godhead – "Christ…the eternal Spirit…God" – were all involved in that sacrifice.

All the many sacrifices offered by the Israelites in the past could not satisfy God. They were but a temporary measure and a faint picture of the One who would come willingly and offer Himself up to God. Our Lord Jesus Christ delighted to do the will of the Father and always sought to please Him. Knowing all that lay ahead and all that it would cost, He set His face steadfastly to go to Jerusalem. His agony and prayer in the Garden of Gethsemane did not represent a conflict of wills – His against the Father's – but rather a statement of His resolve: "O my Father, if it be possible, let this cup pass from me: nevertheless not as I will, but as thou wilt" (Mt 26.39). He was committed to doing all that God required even if it meant that He, the Holy One, must be made sin for us.

He laid down His life

"I am the good shepherd: the good shepherd giveth his life for the sheep … As the Father knoweth me, even so know I the Father: and I lay down my life for the sheep … Therefore doth my Father love me, because I lay down my life, that I might take it again" (Jn 10.11, 15, 17).

The words of the Lord Jesus were not empty promises. When He made His claim to be the Good Shepherd, He based this on the coming reality of His death on behalf of the sheep. The first mention of a shepherd in the Bible is found in Genesis 4 where Abel is said to have been a keeper of sheep. He realized the value of sacrifice and this was demonstrated in his offering to God from the flock. His brother, Cain, preferred to bring the fruit of his own labours from the harvest field. Cain was not ignorant of how to approach God, but in pride he stubbornly tried to come his own way. When God refused his offering, having accepted the offering of Abel, Cain rose up in anger against his brother and killed him. All this was a preview of another Shepherd who would be cruelly slain.

In the history of Israel there were faithful shepherds like David who risked their lives to rescue the sheep. By contrast, there were some who were unfaithful in their task. Instead of feeding the sheep and caring for them, they fleeced them. Facing danger, they fled and left the sheep to be ravaged by the predators. God spoke to them in warning through the prophet Ezekiel: "Son of man, prophesy against the shepherds of Israel…Woe be to the shepherds of Israel that do feed themselves! should not the shepherds feed the flocks?…neither have ye sought that which was lost; but with force and with cruelty have ye ruled them. And they were scattered, because there is no shepherd" (Ezek 34.2, 4-5).

The Lord Jesus was no hireling shepherd, acting only out of self-interest and personal gain. His love and care were true, right to the end. He faced the enemy and laid down His life for us lost and wayward sheep.

He poured out His life
"Therefore will I divide him a portion with the great, and he shall divide the spoil with the strong; because he hath poured out his soul unto death: and he was numbered with the transgressors; and he bare the sin of many, and made intercession for the transgressors" (Isaiah 53.12).

In the opening chapters of the book of Leviticus we read of

various offerings that the Israelites were instructed to bring before God. These pointed forward to the work that Christ would accomplish when He came. The burnt offering reminds us of the pleasure that God found in the death of Christ, when He offered up His life to God; the meal offering suggests the perfection of that life; the peace offering portrays the fellowship we enjoy when we trust in Him; the sin and trespass offerings remind us of our need as sinners being met when He shed His blood for us.

There was another offering called the drink offering. This was poured out completely as an accompanying offering. When Christ poured out His soul unto death for us, He held nothing back.

He sank under God's judgment

"Deep calleth unto deep at the noise of thy waterspouts: all thy waves and thy billows are gone over me" (Ps 42.7).
"I sink in deep mire, where there is no standing: I am come into deep waters, where the floods overflow me" (Ps 69.2).
Many of us have been impressed and even frightened by the awesome power of the sea. In the height of a storm, great ships have been tossed about like corks upon the ocean. Some of these vessels have foundered with the loss of all on board. Men are so often powerless in the face of such overwhelming force.

Surveying the Scriptures, we see a number of miraculous deliverances at sea. On one occasion Jesus was able to sleep in the midst of a storm on Galilee and then rise to calm the wind and waves with a word. On another occasion He walked upon the waves and came to the aid of His fearful disciples. Other examples of rescues at sea include the stories of a faithful apostle, Paul (Acts 27.22-25), and a disobedient prophet, Jonah (Jon 2.9-10): both knew that God's intervention had saved them.

The various writers of the Psalms expressed the depths of their emotions when faced with difficulties and surrounded by enemies. They likened these experiences to great waves that threatened to engulf them, but they too could speak of the deliverance that God brought. The experience of the Lord Jesus Christ at Calvary was different – a cry went unheeded, mercy was withheld and self-survival was out of the question. To become our Saviour, He had to endure the awful suffering upon the cross; He was immersed in the waves of judgment until the full price had been paid. What He accomplished to put away sin by the sacrifice of Himself was a work that was exclusively His own. We could never have any part in it; however, we are now linked to Him by faith and the Scriptures teach that death, crucifixion and a cross should all be known in our spiritual experience too.

Our death with Christ

"Know ye not, that so many of us as were baptized into Jesus Christ were baptized into his death? Therefore we are buried with him by baptism into death: that like as Christ was raised up from the dead by the glory of the Father, even so we also should walk in newness of life ... Now if we be dead with Christ, we believe that we shall also live with him" (Rom 6.3-4, 8).

In Romans 6, Paul was countering the argument that those who had been justified by God's grace might consider themselves to have a licence to sin, to which he replied, "God forbid." He explained that those who have believed in Christ are so closely identified with Him that God sees them as one – they are "baptized into Christ Jesus". He emphasized that having died with Christ, "our old man" (all that we were formerly under the headship of Adam) has been crucified with Him.

If we *know* that Christ has put an end to sin, and we are in Him, then we too are finished with sin: we are to *reckon* ourselves dead to sin and *yield* our members as instruments of righteousness in the service of Christ. We were once in Adam, the head of a sinful and doomed race, but now we have a new head in Christ. We also have a new life and a new power to please God and not ourselves.

In believer's baptism we declare publicly that we have died with Christ, we have been buried with Him, and raised again with Him. The "newness of life" we now enjoy did not commence at our baptism, but rather at the moment of conversion, when we were completely changed and given new desires to live for Christ.

These truths must be appropriated and worked out in daily living. The former sinful habits are to be put to death by forsaking them: "Mortify therefore your members which are upon the earth" (Col 3.5). In a paradoxical way, this is the pathway to life in its fullest dimension: "If ye through the Spirit do mortify the deeds of the body, ye shall live" (Rom 8.13).

Our crucifixion

"I am crucified with Christ: nevertheless I live; yet not I, but Christ liveth in me: and the life which I now live in the flesh I live by the faith of the Son of God, who loved me, and gave himself for me … And they that are Christ's have crucified the flesh with the affections and lusts … But God forbid that I should glory, save in the cross of our Lord Jesus Christ, by whom the world is crucified unto me, and I unto the world" (Gal 2.20; 5.24; 6.14).

Paul was declaring that the world was finished with him and he was finished with it. In a real and practical way he had nailed his own selfish desires to the cross. Aware of the influence of the flesh in his life, he did not indulge it but rather deliberately denied it. (We should remember that the flesh never dies while we are here upon earth; it will always have the potential to drag us down and pull us back.) In another passage, Paul spelt out that the many earthly advantages he had once enjoyed before his conversion and would have taken pride in, were now regarded as of little consequence; indeed, he counted them as loss (Phil 3.7). He would boast of them no longer; his only glory now was the cross.

The pain of crucifixion is unavoidable: there is no easy or comfortable way to undergo it. It is a challenge for us to deliberately nail to the tree, as it were, that which is so appealing to our flesh. Sometimes we might even consider returning to the cross to remove those nails. May the Lord help us to keep them there and not slip back into sin.

Our cross

"And he said to them all, If any man will come after me, let him deny himself, and take up his cross daily, and follow me" (Lk 9.23).

We too have a cross to bear if we would be true disciples of Christ. Sometimes people speak of a difficulty or a chronic problem in their lives; it may be unemployment, bereavement or poor health. They say, "That is my cross, and I will just have to bear it." Our Saviour is not unsympathetic to the trials we pass through, but that is not what He meant. These are problems common to everyone, whether believers or not.

He was issuing a challenge to His disciples, then and now, to follow Him, whatever the cost. A commitment to follow Him presents various challenges to us: a denial of self – that is hard and our spirits resist it; taking up our cross daily – that is painful too because it involves sacrifice and sometimes reproach; following the path He has chosen for us – that path can be rough and uphill. The great compensation in it all is that we will be travelling with Him. This will not mean a grim and austere life bound by misery, but rather true freedom and joy will be ours through wholehearted abandonment to Christ.

We must be careful to keep a balance in our thinking. We can enjoy what God so freely has bestowed upon us, including material blessings and comforts, but we should never live for them. On the other hand, there would be no great virtue in choosing to sleep on a hard bed or refraining from having supper, for example – that would be simply self-denial of a few specific comforts. Christ's words go much deeper than that; the *whole self* is to be denied. This means living, not to please ourselves, but to please God in everything.

We should offer up our lives

"I beseech you therefore, brethren, by the mercies of God, that ye present your bodies a living sacrifice, holy, acceptable unto God, which is your reasonable service" (Rom 12.1).

We are consciously to offer our bodies to God for His service. In view of all that God has done for us in Christ, it is the least that we can do. For some, this is a memorable crisis experience in their lives, particularly if God calls them for special service. For many others this will be a commitment made at the beginning of each day with a prayer for strength to remain true to this resolve.

Our bodies are valuable to God if they are offered to Him. Our thoughts, words and deeds can glorify Him; our lips can speak for Him and our hands work for Him; our feet can advance for Him in the spread of the gospel. Any sacrifice that we make for Him becomes an act of worship; a sweet aroma arises to God and delights His heart.

We should be ready to lay down our lives

"Hereby perceive we the love of God, because he laid down his life for us: and we ought to lay down our lives for the brethren" (1 Jn 3.16). *"Who have for my life laid down their own necks: unto whom not only I give thanks, but also all the churches of the Gentiles"* (Rom 16.4).

Laying down our lives means that we sacrificially serve others. This is what the Lord did. He saw us in our need and He answered it by setting His own life to the side so that He might attend to ours. We may not be called upon to die for others, although some choice saints have willingly done this very thing, but we are to seek to be a blessing to others, even if it means disregarding our own needs.

In the last chapter of his letter to the Romans, Paul recalled the willingness of Aquila and Priscilla to lay down their "neck" (singular in the original) by risking their lives for him. Not only were they united and devoted to one another in their marriage, but also they were as one in their love to others. When Paul recalled their faithful support, he was moved to give thanks to God. We could never have enough couples like Aquila and Priscilla!

We should pour out our lives
"For I am now ready to be offered [poured out], and the time of my departure is at hand" (2 Tim 4.6).

In the last letter that Paul wrote before his execution in Rome, he struck a confident note. His life had been a full one: it was full of trials and full of joys. It was also a fulfilled one. Having completed the work God had given him to do, he was ready to leave this world and to depart to be with Christ. He had no regrets and no need to linger as nothing had been left undone. He had been bold and brave in battle for the Lord. He had run eagerly in the Christian race, unencumbered by unnecessary weights, and he had kept to the rules. Focused on the One who awaited him at the finish, he was entering the last leg of the marathon with keen anticipation. The things God had entrusted to him had been faithfully guarded and passed on to others. Death held no fears for him – he was going home! His final act would be sacrificial: for the sake of Christ, he was going to lay his head upon the block. Like Stephen, the first martyr, Paul would not only die for Christ but also die like Christ.

It is good to be ready. Paul was prepared to be poured out upon the altar like a drink offering. Many godly men have set an example for us: showing us not only how to live, but also how to die.

We will never sink under God's judgment!
"And their sins and iniquities will I remember no more" (Heb 10.17). *"And to wait for his Son from heaven, whom he raised from the dead, even Jesus, which delivered us from the wrath to come"* (1 Thes 1.10).
We have thought of Christ's death for us and how we can be like Him in our daily experience (offering up, laying down and pouring out our own lives). But there is one important difference

– we will never have to sink under the judgment of the wrath of God. Christ has borne all that for us, and our sins and iniquities are all forgiven. This amazing truth fills our hearts with joy.

A PERSONAL REMINDER
To become more like Christ, I must:
- offer up my life to God
- die to self and to sin
- bear my cross daily.

CHAPTER 12

His Resurrection and Ascension

The foundation of our faith is not a creed but a living person, Jesus Christ, the Son of God. According to the Scriptures, He died and was buried (1 Cor 15.3-4). Had that been the end, our faith would be in vain and we would be the most miserable of men, no more than mourning pilgrims to a tomb (1 Cor 15.17-19).

It was not the end at all, but a glorious beginning when Christ arose from the dead as the mighty Conqueror (1 Cor 15.20). He triumphed over sin, death and the grave. The bondage of sin was broken for ever, the sting of death was removed, and the apparent victory of the grave was made null and void. When Christ came out from the tomb, He did so in a real, recognizable but glorified body. That makes Christ's resurrection unique: others had died and been raised to life, but none like the Saviour: they died again, but He lives for ever. Having ascended to heaven, He presently sits at the Father's right hand in glory.

Clear Prediction
When Christ was telling the disciples of His impending death, He linked it to the truth of His resurrection, that "He must go unto Jerusalem, and suffer many things of the elders and chief priests and scribes, and be killed, and be raised again the third day" (Mt 16.21-23; Mk 8. 31-33; Lk 9.22). If the first part of the statement caused them dismay, the second part should have comforted them, but it seems that they did not understand. He had already claimed to be the resurrection and the life, and the

source of blessing to those who would receive Him. He had promised the sign of the prophet Jonah and judgment to those who would reject Him (Mt 16.4). Furthermore, His enemies were told that even if they destroyed the temple of His body, He would raise it up again (Jn 2.19).

On the day of Pentecost, Peter quoted from the Scriptures (Acts 2.27; Ps 16.10) where it was foretold that God's Holy One who would not remain in *sheol* (the place of departed spirits after death), nor see corruption. Christ's resurrection fulfilled this Old Testament prophecy.

United Testimony

There is a sound, historical basis to what we believe. We have good reason to accept that the four Gospel writers were faithful in recounting in their own manner what they had seen and heard, or had revealed to them by the Spirit of God. They were nearer than anyone else to the events that took place and certain features have the stamp of authenticity: differences were left unaltered; gaps were left unfilled; they were remarkably honest about the disciples' unbelief; they were notably restrained concerning their joy. Certain difficulties appear to surface when we try to harmonize the four accounts, but a reasonable attempt at a single story line can be achieved by anyone who takes the time to study the Gospels. Details that are not so clear are never so crucial as to seriously prejudice the final verdict.

It is more important to grasp something of the freshness and spontaneity portrayed by the biblical records of that tumultuous day. No attempt was made by the writers to contrive identical accounts and there was nothing ponderous in their style. More in the manner of on-the-spot reporters, they recorded with almost breathless amazement, the hurrying to and fro, the tears and the joy, the incredulity of the friends of Christ and the shock of His enemies.

No one saw Christ in the act of rising from the dead. Then what did witnesses see? It is recorded by the four Gospel writers that several women and disciples were amazed to discover an empty tomb. The graveclothes and separate headcloth were the only remaining vestiges of the burial. Soon afterwards, they saw the risen Lord Himself, and in the days following Christ appeared to His own on a number of occasions.

The enemies of Christ had taken every precaution to prevent anything unusual happening. A deep spear wound had been inflicted by the soldiers after Christ died. After the body was taken down from the cross, it was prepared for burial by His followers. In accordance with the custom of the day, it was wrapped in cloth bands and anointed with spices. After being interred in a tomb hewn out of solid rock, three measures were instituted by the authorities to ensure that the body would remain there: the entrance was covered by a large rolling stone; this was sealed; and guards were posted; however, the stone, the seal and the soldiers would not be enough.

The Gospel writers were characteristically frank about the disbelief that clung to some of the followers of Christ after the empty tomb was discovered. Peter could only gaze in wonderment short of comprehension (Lk 24.12). Mary feared that the body had been snatched from the grave and taken away (Jn 20.13). The disciples thought that the words of the women were like idle tales (Lk 24.11). Thomas refused to accept the story on hearsay (Jn 20.25). Mark mentions three times that there was plain disbelief (Mk 16.11, 13-14). Thankfully, this was quickly swept away by the reality of His presence amongst them. Joy flooded their souls and a mighty power and boldness soon replaced the weakness and fear that had marked them only days before.

The Jewish leaders were in a panic to hold back the truth, and again bribery was the option that came readily to their minds (Mt 28.11-15). They put about a false rumour that the body had been stolen, the very thing they had tried to prevent (Mt 27.64).

Many Witnesses

Christ made at least ten appearances to His followers in the forty day period between His resurrection and ascension to heaven. Half of these occurred on the first day of the week, the day of resurrection. John implies that there were other times when He was with believers (Jn 20.30) and Paul mentions over five hundred people seeing Him at once (1 Cor 15.6). On each occasion the Lord met a particular human need. He remains the same today, the answer to our every need.

For Mary Magdalene, Christ dried her tears. She was found alone weeping before the empty tomb. The depth of her grief could not be shared. She had concluded that the body of her Lord had been taken away and she was distraught. Overwhelmed by sadness, she did not recognize the man who spoke to her; but when He used her own name, she suddenly realized it was her Lord. There followed a sweet reunion (Jn 20.11-18; Mk 16.9-11). It was Christ alone who fully understood her burdens and grief and it was only He who could pour in the comfort and restore the joy. Our extremity is still His opportunity. There were other faithful women who were devoted to their Lord; when they met the risen Christ, they held Him by the feet and poured out their hearts in adoring worship (Mt 28.1-10). They became the first heralds of the resurrection.

The Lord also appeared personally to Peter, the disciple who had denied Him (Lk 24.34; 1 Cor 15.5). What marvellous grace that this should have been so! Bitter tears of repentance had been shed and Christ forgave his backsliding. Another encounter took place that same day with two friends who were walking to the village of Emmaus. It would have been hard to meet a more forlorn and dejected pair. Their hopes of a conquering redeemer had been dashed and when they first heard the report of the women who had seen the empty tomb and heard the angelic message, they remained stubbornly unconvinced. The Stranger who drew near and journeyed with them on the road upbraided them for their unbelief and began to instruct them from the Scriptures. When He became their guest and started to eat with them, they recognized Him as their Lord. He opened their eyes and warmed their hearts (Lk 24.13-35).

Behind a closed door, ten men were gathered, petrified with fear. They believed that the Jews could as easily do to them what they had just done to Jesus. In a miraculous way the Lord appeared in their midst and showed them the fresh scars of His wounded hands and side. One can imagine the joy flooding in and the smiles breaking out. He had dispelled their fears and brought peace to their hearts (Jn 20.19-23). Thomas had been absent on that occasion. He was sceptical about their report, but after eight days the Lord reappeared to them all and removed his doubts (Jn 20.26-29). There was also a special appearance to James, the Lord's brother, who had previously been in unbelief (1 Cor 15.7).

After the crucifixion, seven disciples had gone back to fishing, but their best efforts went unrewarded. Christ then appeared to them and guided their labours, resulting in a large catch of fish (Jn 21.1-14). Christ had a greater work for them all to do when, soon afterwards, He commanded them to begin spreading His word and fishing for men. To enable them to engage in this highest of endeavours, He promised His presence (Mt 28.16-20). Finally, from the Mount of Olives, He promised His power as they would go and carry the gospel message to every corner of the earth (Lk 24.50-52; Acts 1.8-9).

From that same mountain He ascended and a cloud received Him out of their sight. The words of the two angels brought comfort and hope: "Ye men of Galilee, why stand ye gazing up into heaven? this same Jesus, which is taken up from you into heaven, shall so come in like manner as ye have seen him go into heaven" (Acts 1.11). What wonderful words – "this same Jesus". He would return and be physically recognizable, but also He would be unchanged in His love, mercy and grace. After He ascended to heaven, others like Stephen, Paul and John would be privileged to catch a sight of Him in glory, even while they were still alive upon earth.

Bold Preaching

The book of the Acts pulsates with energy and glows with heat. There is nothing half-hearted or lukewarm in the book. The message of the risen Lord was carried with zeal and boldness to every place by the servants of Christ (Acts 1.22). They spoke as men renewed; the Lord was alive!

Peter's message to the Jews was forthright: they had crucified their Messiah, but God had raised Him from the dead. These two notes were struck repeatedly: "Jesus of Nazareth ... ye have taken and by wicked hands have crucified and slain: whom God hath raised up" (2.22-24); "you killed the Prince of life, whom God hath raised from the dead" (3.15); "Jesus Christ of Nazareth, whom ye crucified, whom God raised from the dead" (4.10); "The God of our fathers raised up Jesus, whom ye slew and hanged on a tree" (5.30). And yet, Peter did not leave the Jews merely stricken in conscience; in all that he said there was a gracious note of appeal and also a welcoming invitation of pardon. He called on them to repent, believe and be blessed. Salvation was to be found only through faith in none other than Jesus of Nazareth. Peter and the other apostles presented the message boldly, simply and directly and many were amazed, noting that those simple Galileans "had been with Jesus" (4.13). No, they had not been visiting a tomb; they had just been communing with their risen Lord. The words they spoke were fresh and fragrant with His presence.

Paul's preaching added further truth concerning the risen Christ. The Athenians were to hear of a coming judgment which was confirmed by the resurrection (17.31). On several occasions

Paul gave a personal testimony concerning his conversion to Christ. He never lost his sense of wonder at the grace of God intervening in his life when the risen Christ confronted him on the Damascus road. Before a mixed crowd of Sadducees and Pharisees, and before Felix, he spoke of his hope of personal resurrection (23.6; 24.15). He argued cogently before King Agrippa that God's power made resurrection credible (26.8). The resurrection was a fulfilment of what the Old Testament had clearly foretold concerning the Saviour and, after all, Paul had seen Him (26.23).

Faithful Teaching

The New Testament epistles are rich with instruction concerning Christ's resurrection. If we draw the various strands together we see that a number of great truths are based on this cardinal teaching. The resurrection was a demonstration of God's power. Paul prayed that the Christians in Ephesus might enter into a deeper knowledge of the lofty purposes of God for their lives, referring to the "working of his mighty power, which he wrought in Christ, when he raised him from the dead, and set him at his own right hand in the heavenly places" (Eph 1.19-20). It was also a vindication of Christ's person and work: He was "declared to be the Son of God with power ... by the resurrection from the dead" (Rom 1.4); furthermore, "God also hath highly exalted him, and given him a name which is above every name" (Phil 2.9). Christ's resurrection was the ultimate victory that assures us that He is all He ever claimed to be. Furthermore, the resurrection was an evidence of the Spirit's quickening; the same "Spirit of him that raised up Jesus from the dead" dwells in us (Rom 8.11).

For us who believe, Christ's resurrection is also the assurance of coming glory. In 1 Corinthians 15, the classic exposition of resurrection truth, Paul showed that all our hopes are inextricably linked with Christ. Christ is the firstfruits of a coming great harvest and His resurrection is the assurance that we too shall be raised, changed and fitted for heaven (1 Cor

6.14). The wonder of it is that we shall be like Him and bear the image of the heavenly (1 Cor 15.49). For those who are unrepentant and refuse to believe, the resurrection of Christ is a confirmation of coming judgment, as we have noted above. Finally, it is a prelude to Satan's total defeat (1 Cor 15.25; Col 2.15).

Daily Living

An appreciation of Christ and His resurrection opens up for us a great storehouse of divine resources and blessing. We can and should know something of daily communion with the risen Christ, through prayer and reading of His Word. Paul's great desire was to "know him and the power of his resurrection" (Phil 3.10). With this communion comes an assurance that all is well with our souls and we are accepted before God because Christ was "raised again for our justification" (Rom 4.25). We enjoy the forgiveness of sins, for God, who raised Him from the dead, has quickened us together with Him, having forgiven us all trespasses (Col 2.12-13). Instead of the coming wrath, we wait to see God's Son from heaven, "whom he raised from the dead, even Jesus" (1 Thes 1.10).

There was a terrible bondage associated with the law and sin. The law exposed sin but had no power to free man from sin's guilt and power. But through the resurrection of Christ, we can know liberty and new life in Him; we are no longer bound by the law but joined to another, "even to him who is raised from the dead, that we should bring forth fruit unto God" (Rom 7.4); "Like as Christ was raised up from the dead by the glory of the Father, even so we also should walk in newness of life. For if we have been planted together in the likeness of his death, we shall be also in the likeness of his resurrection" (Rom 6.4-5).

The resurrection of Christ has made available to us who believe an almighty power which God "wrought in Christ, when he raised him from the dead" (Eph 1.20). That power operates to elevate and enrich us because He "hath quickened us together with Christ ... and hath raised us up together, and made us sit together in heavenly places", the place of spiritual blessings (Eph 2.6). Paul experienced God's protecting power and deliverance in his own life in the midst of great pressure: "we had the sentence of death in ourselves, that we should not trust in ourselves, but in God which raiseth the dead" (2 Cor 1.9). Paul knew too that at the right hand of God there was a divine intercessor, "Christ ... that is risen again, who is even at the right hand of God, who also maketh intercession for us" (Rom 8.34).

Belief in the resurrection is an integral part of our faith. You are saved, said Paul, if you confess with your mouth Jesus as Lord and believe in your heart "that God hath raised him from the dead" (Rom 10.9). Peter tells us that God raised Him from the dead, and gave him glory; that our faith and hope might be in God (1 Pet 1.21). When we exercise that faith day by day, there is growth and conformity to Christ. Paul longed to know more of "the power of his resurrection ... being made conformable unto his death" (Phil 3.10). We should, therefore, become more heavenly-minded even while still on earth: "If ye then be risen with Christ, seek those things which are above, where Christ sitteth on the right hand of God" (Col 3.1).

Finally, the resurrection gives us hope. The risen Lord is coming back; "The dead in Christ shall rise first: Then we which are alive and remain shall be caught up together with them in the clouds to meet the Lord in the air" (1Thes 4.16-17); God "hath begotten us again unto a lively hope, by the resurrection of Jesus Christ from the dead, to an inheritance incorruptible and undefiled, and that fadeth not away, reserved in heaven for you" (1 Pet 1.3-4). We too shall be raised and ascend to heaven to be with Him in glory for ever.

The writer to the Hebrews describes our hope as being "sure and stedfast", and an anchor for our souls (Heb 6.19-20). In the early days of sailing ships, a small auxiliary boat carrying the anchor of the main ship was sent ahead during a storm. It was called 'the forerunner'. Once it made its way through the breakers into the calm of the harbour, the anchor was laid. The larger ship was thus secured to the anchor inside the haven. That is exactly what Christ has done for us. As our Forerunner, He has braved the storm and entered into the presence of God in heaven, ahead of us. Because He is already there, we can rest assured that we will arrive safely home too. Our souls are anchored in Him, our risen exalted Lord.

A PERSONAL REMINDER
To become more like Christ, I must:
- be a faithful witness
- walk daily in the power of a new life
- remember I am going home.

CHAPTER 13

Our Shepherd

The Lord Jesus Christ has the power not only to save us but also to keep us and sustain us on the journey home to heaven. That journey is not always smooth; there are difficulties on the pathway that must be faced and overcome. We are prone to stray and so we need a shepherd; because we often struggle with trials, we need a priest; when we sin, we need an advocate; and when we sorrow, we need a friend. Christ fulfils all of these roles and more for the blessing of His people, excelling all others who have gone before. He alone is the Great Shepherd, the Great High Priest, the righteous Advocate and the faithful Friend. His work on the cross is over but His work upon the throne is ongoing. Presently He sits at the right hand of God in heaven and He is there for us. He is interested in all that we do and He has the power to help us day by day.

The work of shepherding is demanding. Sheep are wayward and prone to wander; they need constant supervision. Good pasture and fresh water are daily requirements. Then there are predators that would attack the flock, scattering and devouring them; therefore, protection is vital. The same holds true in the spiritual realm when we think of the varied needs of God's flock.

There are examples in the Scriptures of those who were faithful shepherds like David. He never left the flock unattended, even when he was called away. His eldest brother, Eliab, called them just "a few sheep" but to David every sheep was precious (1 Sam 17.28, 34-37). On one occasion a lion attacked and carried away one of the lambs; David risked his life to rescue it. The lessons he learned on the hillsides were training for the greater task that lay ahead of him when he would lead the nation of Israel as their king.

There were others who failed in their responsibility to lead God's people. These were described by Ezekiel (ch 34) as shepherds who put their own interests first. God dismissed them and vowed that instead He would care for His people. When the patriarch, Jacob, spoke to his sons before his death, his words referring to Joseph contained the prophecy of a coming One: "His bow abode in strength, and the arms of his hands were made strong by the hands of the mighty God of Jacob; (from thence is the shepherd, the stone of Israel)" (Gen 49.24). Christ was the fulfilment of all these words: He was the Shepherd who was smitten by the very same people He loved and cared for; He was the rejected Stone who was set aside by the nation of Israel. But today, Christ is the true Shepherd of all those who believe on Him and follow Him. We know Him too as the foundation stone of our faith and the chief corner stone in the building which is His Church.

The Good Shepherd
In John's Gospel, chapter 10, the Lord is seen as the Good Shepherd. Christ acted on behalf of his Father and for His pleasure. He spoke of "*my Father*" and thus proclaimed His deity: "I and my Father are one" (v 30). He shared a constant fellowship with the Father that made Him fully aware of God's will – He must die for the sheep and rise again from the dead. Christ's subjection to that will made Him the object of the Father's love (v 17). The Father and the Son were always of one mind and heart concerning the great plan of salvation.

He also spoke of "*my life*" (v 15), and we are reminded of its sufficiency. That life was one of holiness and perfection, but no less was demanded by God when Christ laid down His life for the sheep. His voluntary act in giving Himself as a sacrifice brought satisfaction to God and made salvation possible for us.

In the expression, *"my sheep"* (v 14), we learn of the intimacy that Christ has with those who belong to Him. Having laid down His life for them, He looks upon them with a holy jealousy and cares for them constantly. He is not like those who were hired to care for the sheep but fled at the first sign of danger. When He spoke of *"my voice"* (v 16), He described His authority to guide and direct the sheep: "My sheep hear my voice, and I know them, and they follow me" (v 27). We know the voice of the One who cares for us and we can confidently do His bidding and take the path that He chooses for us. There are many other voices of "strangers" that would lure us away from the path of blessing; we would be wise to refuse them.

The eternal security of those who belong to Christ was so clearly expressed when He spoke of *"my hand"*: "I give unto them eternal life; and they shall never perish, neither shall any man pluck them out of my hand" (v 28). We should restate this glorious truth in every generation: those who trust in Christ are safe forever and they can never be lost. It is possible for careless Christians to lose their joy and their testimony. God has disciplined some who have lost their health and their life here upon earth – He has taken them home early (1 Cor 11.30). Furthermore, they can lose their heavenly reward, but, thank God, they can never lose their salvation. All of us who believe in Him are in His hand and in the Father's hand, doubly safe and that for ever.

He seeks us
In John 10 it is clear that the Good Shepherd is constantly seeking to bring other sheep into the flock: "And other sheep I have, which are not of this fold: them also I must bring, and they shall hear my voice; and there shall be one fold, and one shepherd" (v 16). Although He came first to the nation of Israel, the love of the Lord Jesus Christ has been extended to the

Gentiles. Today, from all over the world, God is calling out of the nations a people for His Name (Acts 15.14).

The shepherd of Luke 15 valued every sheep. He left the ninety-nine sheep and went out to seek diligently for the one which was missing (v 4). He sought it until he found it, and then he bore it safely home. What a joyous celebration he and his friends had! Here too we have a picture of the heart of Christ. Later on we read of the Saviour's words to Zacchaeus: "For the Son of Man is come to seek and to save that which was lost" (Lk 19.10).

He leads us
Shepherds in the western world often use sheepdogs to herd their flocks. Standing at a distance from the sheep and using hand or voice signals, they control their dogs so that the sheep are moved in the appropriate direction. The shepherds in the east are different; they will more often lead the flock than drive them. They go before and face any obstacles or dangers first (Isa 48.17). This is what Christ has done; during His time upon earth He experienced all the trials of the way, sin apart. Today He knows what lies ahead of us. If we seek to follow Him and to be obedient to His voice, He will teach us many valuable lessons, through the good times as well as through the difficult ones.

He feeds us
Christ is the food of His people (Jn 6.35). This means that He satisfies our souls, and when we feed upon Him and His word, we grow strong. In the natural sphere, not a day goes by that we do not need to eat. It is no different in the spiritual realm. We should come to the Scriptures daily with a desire to seek and an expectation to find Christ on every page. When we learn something new about Him, we can turn that thought over in our minds and enjoy it in our hearts. But even familiar truths will fortify us as we seek to live for Him day by day. The more we are occupied with Him, the more like Him we will become. He refreshes us.

David spoke of the Lord as his shepherd in Psalm 23: "He leadeth me beside the still waters. He restoreth my soul" (vv 2-3). We can become tired and jaded at times. Some days are difficult and problems can seem insurmountable; however, the weary in spirit can be refreshed by time spent with Him. No one understands us like He does and no one is able to help us as He can. He brings peace and calm to the troubled mind and heart. When we spend time alone with Him, we begin to see the problems of earth from a different perspective, and we are able to carry on.

There were occasions when the Lord Jesus urged His disciples to come apart and rest for a while (Mk 6.31). He knew that His work could be physically, mentally and emotionally demanding. They had their limits and they needed to recuperate and regain their strength and vigour.

He protects us

The Lord Jesus loved His disciples so much that He never failed to warn them of the dangers ahead. He knew that erroneous teaching could destroy the flock: "Beware of false prophets, which come to you in sheep's clothing, but inwardly they are ravening wolves" (Mt 7.15). His followers could expect violent opposition: "Beware of men: for they will deliver you up to the councils, and they will scourge you in their synagogues" (Mt 10.17). The Pharisees were a constant threat and their hypocrisy could easily spread and contaminate the lives of God's children: "Beware ye of the leaven of the Pharisees, which is hypocrisy" (Lk 12.1). He warned the disciples also to beware of the pride of the scribes who loved prominence and ostentation (Mk 12.38).

There were other dangers too, such as materialism, that could weaken the flock of God: "Take heed, and beware of covetousness: for a man's life consisteth not in the abundance of the things which he possesseth" (Lk 12.15). For these many reasons, Christ urged vigilance and trust in God: "Watch and pray" (Mt 26.41; Mk 13.33).

He lifts up the fallen and broken

All of us can stumble upon the pathway and fall by the way. Just like Peter, our profession of loyalty often runs far ahead of our true commitment and we come up short when the pressure is increased. The Lord Jesus is aware of all of our failings and yet He still loves us. He prayed for Peter and appeared to him after the resurrection, when He forgave him. Peter was restored to a place of useful service. Even when Christians fall into gross sin, failure is never total, and our Lord is ever willing to receive the repentant into close fellowship with Himself once again.

There are those who have been broken by sin and wounded on the pathway of life. The Lord specializes in mending and restoring that which has been broken (Lk 4.18; Isa 61.1). The Gospels bring before us a number of people who had been completely given over to lives of sin – until they met Him! Such a woman had been Mary Magdalene who was possessed with seven demons, but Christ healed her completely (Mk 16.9; Lk 8.2)). No case was too difficult for Him.

He carries the young

Lambs need special care and sometimes they need to be carried. The prophet, Isaiah, spoke of the tenderness and gentleness of God's Servant: "He shall feed his flock like a shepherd: he shall gather the lambs with his arm, and carry them in his bosom, and shall gently lead those that are with young" (Isa 40.11). Even in a physical sense, the Lord Jesus delighted to take up the young children in His arms and bless them; the disciples would have chased them away. He revealed that the secret to being in His kingdom was to have the simple, unquestioning faith of a young child (Mk 10.14-16).

Our responsibilities

The Lord Jesus still calls for those with shepherd hearts to seek the lost and to look after His people. What does it mean to have a shepherd heart? It means to care deeply for others and always to act in their interests. When the love of Christ takes hold of one's heart, there is a constant burden to reach out to the lost with the good news of the gospel. One is engaging in a divine rescue mission, no less. There is no worthier way to pass the brief years of life down here than to spend and be spent so that others might hear and believe.

When, by the grace of God, people come to trust in Christ, there is the need to care for them and nourish them with the Word of God. It is hardly enough just to buy them a new Bible and tell them to keep coming to the meetings of the Christians. There needs to be personal involvement on the part of those who would shepherd them and this always proves costly in terms of time and effort. There are no short cuts; sometimes, there can be disappointments. As new believers grow in grace and in the knowledge of the truth, they begin to understand their responsibilities. There is a need for them to be baptized as a public sign of allegiance to Christ, and then a further need for them to share in the fellowship of a local church.

Every local assembly of Christians needs shepherds. In the Bible these men are also called "elders" or "overseers". The first word emphasizes their maturity and the second their responsibility. They are not elected to a position by a popular vote, but the Holy Spirit raises them up. They are godly men of spiritual experience who lead by example; others will recognize this. The Lord Jesus expects that they will be like Him by acting even as He acted.

Christ spoke to Peter after His resurrection and commanded him to feed His sheep and lambs (Jn 21.15-17). The word "feed" in this context means more than just providing food. It has a wider application and covers all aspects of the flock's care. The apostle never forgot the words of the risen Lord and the two letters he wrote later to help God's people reflected his past experiences.

Peter knew that those to whom he wrote had been wayward

and gone astray in their sins, but they had returned to Christ who had saved them. Peter described Him as "the Shepherd and Bishop (overseer)" of their souls (1 Pet 2.25). He reminded the elders who sought to look after the flock of God that their motives had to be pure. He was aware that personal advancement and even enrichment had motivated some; others had abused their position by ruling through force rather than by example. After such necessary warnings, he brought a word of encouragement for elders everywhere: "And when the chief Shepherd shall appear, ye shall receive a crown of glory that fadeth not away" (1 Pet 5.4). There would be a special reward for those who had shepherded well. Implicit in these words was the realization that one day the elders would be required to give an account to God of their stewardship amongst God's people.

Whilst Peter's emphasis was on the shepherds and their personal character, Paul had a burden to strengthen them in view of the dangers that would lie ahead. This was evident when he addressed the elders of the church at Ephesus for the last time: "Take heed therefore unto yourselves, and to all the flock, over the which the Holy Ghost hath made you overseers, to feed the church of God, which he hath purchased with his own blood. For I know this, that after my departing shall grievous wolves enter in among you, not sparing the flock. Also of your own selves shall men arise, speaking perverse things, to draw away disciples after them" (Acts 20.28-30).

Paul anticipated that there would be attacks from without and challenges from within. Some evil men would seek to take advantage, after the apostle had left the Christians, by forcing their way into the church to destroy it. More subtle attacks would arise from those within the community of believers who would begin to teach error. These false teachers would seek to gain a following and divide the people of God; therefore, the shepherds needed to be men of resolute determination who would defend and protect the flock against such attacks.

Paul had a love and care for "all the churches" (2 Cor 11.28). There were the good, the bad and, yes, even the ugly – churches that had strayed far from the truth of God. His life would have been simpler and easier by far had he limited his attention to spiritually healthy assemblies of Christians. Why did he bother at all with churches marked by moral problems, doctrinal confusion and disorderly practices? The reason was that he loved them.

Paul recognized in his young associate, Timothy, the right spiritual calibre to lead God's people. Words of encouragement were offered: "Let no man despise thy youth; but be thou an example of the believers, in word, in conversation, in charity, in spirit, in faith, in purity ... Take heed unto thyself, and unto the doctrine; continue in them: for in doing this thou shalt both save thyself, and them that hear thee" (1 Tim 4.12,16). Once again, we see the importance of being a good example. Timothy was exhorted to be brave in the battle, faithful in his stewardship, impartial in his ministry and irreproachable in his testimony. He was to exhibit the features of Christ: "But thou, O man of God, flee these things; and follow after righteousness, godliness, faith, love, patience, meekness" (1 Tim 6.11).

Elders are not the only ones with the responsibility to care. We are all to love one another, look out for one another and care for one another. We may not hold any recognized position in an assembly of Christians but all of us, male and female alike, can assist in many different ways, so that the flock is nurtured and protected. This will bring much pleasure to our Lord's heart and glory to His Name.

A PERSONAL REMINDER
To become more like Christ, I must:
- feed and care for the people of God
- protect them from harm and danger
- lead by example.

CHAPTER 14

Our Great High Priest

A priest represents God before men and men before God. He stands between the two, as it were, and is in touch with both. He is able to bless God and also bring blessing to men, as did Melchisedec (Gen 14.19-20). Moses' brother, Aaron, was named as the first high priest in the nation of Israel and following his death, his descendants filled this role. By contrast, the Lord Jesus Christ is described as our Great High Priest, a title that is uniquely His own.

Christ is perfectly qualified to be our Great High Priest. He was God manifest in flesh. His divine holiness was never compromised by sin, and yet His true humanity was clear for all to see. He experienced trials and sufferings in a way that gave Him a deep sympathy for us, and an understanding of our needs. He knew what it was to be tired, hungry and thirsty. He sorrowed at the death of loved ones. He faced opposition and rejection. All this and more qualified Him to be the One who can truly represent us – He knows us through and through.

Presently He is seated at the Father's right hand where He is active on our behalf. The author of the Epistle to the Hebrews uses this expression, "the right hand", on four occasions. His main aim in writing was to encourage Christians who had been converted from Judaism but who had since come under persecution. Some of them might have been tempted to go back to the visible and ceremonial rituals in their former religion, but the writer showed them that what they had in Christ was better and greater than anything they had ever experienced in Judaism.

These four references to "the right hand" cover the past, present and future work of Christ. In the first reference (Heb 1.3), the writer looked back to the work of Christ upon the cross. He described it as making purification for sins. Having perfectly completed that work to God's satisfaction, Christ set Himself down at the right hand, the place of honour and authority, affection and acceptance. Then, secondly, Christ is said to be "an high priest, who is set on the right hand of the throne of the Majesty in the heavens" (Heb 8.1) where His ministry is to represent and support us; this is His present work for us today. Thirdly, there is a future day of glory implied when we read of Him having offered one sacrifice for sins for ever and having sat down on the right hand of God, "from henceforth expecting till his enemies be made his footstool" (Heb 10.13).

In the final reference (Heb 12.2), the past, present and future are all encompassed, and we are encouraged as we run our "race" to focus upon Him: "Looking unto Jesus the author and finisher of our faith; who for the joy that was set before him endured the cross, despising the shame, and is set down at the right hand of the throne of God." What He started in the beginning as the author of our faith, He is presently perfecting as our representative; He will complete it in a coming day as the finisher of our faith. It is as if He is standing there at the finishing line, urging us to keep going on in the Christian race and to be strong, right until the end.

The example of Aaron
Aaron, the brother of Moses, became the first high priest in Israel. In his official capacity he stood between the people and their God. He had exclusive privileges: only He could enter into the innermost compartment of the tabernacle called the Holy of Holies where God dwelt. The ordinary Israelite was denied that privilege. Even so, Aaron could only stand before

the mercy seat on one day of the year, the great Day of Atonement. On that day he had to bring the blood of a sacrifice for his own sins before he could act on behalf of the people and their sins. The following year the same solemn ritual had to be repeated. From the priesthood and ministry of Aaron we learn many valuable lessons: God is holy and for sinful man to appear before Him a sacrifice must be offered and blood must be shed.

We can hardly think of the many sacrifices that Aaron and his sons offered without contrasting them with the infinitely superior sacrifice of Christ. The unending routine of daily, weekly and yearly sacrifices in the tabernacle or temple could never take away sins. The writer to the Hebrews emphasizes the "once for all" nature of the work of Christ. He tells us that Christ has become a high priest of good things to come and "by his own blood he entered in once into the holy place, having obtained eternal redemption for us" (Heb 9.11-12); "But now once in the end of the world hath he appeared to put away sin by the sacrifice of himself" (Heb 9.26).

The Scriptures, ever frank and transparent, reveal the inadequacy in Aaron himself. Yes, he had many sterling qualities, but in reading through his story we must confess that he had also glaring personal weaknesses. He was carnal and he sinned; he was mortal and he died. His ministry was temporal, and therefore it had to be transferred to another. It could never fulfil God's ultimate purpose for mankind in bringing sinners close to Himself. Only Christ could accomplish this.

The example of Melchisedec
The priesthood of Christ today is after a higher order – the order of Melchisedec. He appears suddenly in the Genesis record (Gen 14.17-24) and disappears just as abruptly. His record in Scripture was unusual in that details of his lineage, birth and death were all omitted. Unusual too was the fact that he functioned as both a king and a priest. Apart from another reference in a short

prophetic psalm (Ps 110), the remaining teaching about him is found in the Epistle to the Hebrews. There much is made of the order of priesthood that he established and which Christ fulfilled. Six times we read of Christ as a priest for ever, "after the order of Melchisedec" (Heb 5.6, 10; 6.20; 7.11, 17, 21).

What was the nature of Melchisedec's ministry? He strengthened Abraham (then called simply Abram) to face and overcome a great trial that lay ahead. Abraham was returning from a battle, victorious but no doubt exhausted. Lot, his nephew, had been rescued and his possessions had been recovered. What Abraham did not know was that in his weakened state, the evil king of Sodom would confront him and tempt him with an inviting proposition, to keep the recovered goods for himself but give up the people to his control.

With perfect timing, Melchisedec reached Abraham first and did five specific things: he blessed Abraham; he blessed God; he gave Abraham bread; he gave him wine; he gave him words. Abraham acknowledged Melchisedec's greatness and superiority by honouring him with a tenth of all that he had brought back. Strengthened by the bread, cheered by the wine and encouraged by the words, Abraham was able to overcome the king of Sodom's temptation. The words he had heard from the mouth of Melchisedec were the same words he was able to repeat in resisting the temptation of the evil king: "I have lift up mine hand unto the Lord, the most high God, the possessor of heaven and earth …" (Gen 14.19-20, 22).

The significance of this today is that we have One in heaven who knows every trial that lies ahead of us. He is touched with the feeling of our infirmities and He is able to succour us and take us through safely to the end (Heb 4.15; 2.18). Indeed, He has unlimited resources from which we can draw. He appears in God's presence for us and prays for us: "He ever liveth to make intercession" (Heb 7.25). We are encouraged to come directly before Him at any time and in any difficulty; He will hear us and freely give us the mercy and grace we need to go on (Heb 4.16). The way is open for immediate access to a personal audience before the throne of grace. He also presents our praise to God at the Father's right hand. His presence in heaven is the foundation for our sure hope that we too shall enter there (Heb 13.15; 6.18-20). Furthermore, as pictured in Melchisedec, this ministry of Christ's is eternal and will never change or be passed on to another.

Our Priesthood

Every child of God is a priest before God (1 Pet 2.5, 9; Rev 1.6; 5.10). We can bless God by loving Him, worshipping Him and serving Him. We can also be a blessing to others by helping and strengthening them in many different ways: praying for them; showing them kindness; and supporting them when they face difficulties.

The key thought in priesthood is the *offering of sacrifices*. God is looking for that which is costly from us and when we give to Him from a full heart, then a sweet smell arises before Him. Let us think of some of the sacrifices that we can offer to Him.

The Sacrifice of our Possessions

The Christians in Philippi were kind. They sent a generous gift to Paul and he wrote a letter to thank them, describing their gift as "an odour of a sweet smell acceptable, wellpleasing to God" (Phil 4.18). Here is the principle of priesthood in action: their love and devotion to God (they blessed God) was expressed in their sacrificial giving to the apostle (they blessed men). As a result, Paul was able to thank both God and them for the bounty he had received.

In the book of the Acts, Paul incorporated the words of the Lord Jesus into his final address to the Ephesian elders: "I have shewed you all things, how that so labouring ye ought to support the weak, and to remember the words of the Lord Jesus, how he said, It is more blessed to give than to receive" (Acts 20.35). These precise words are not found in the Gospels, but Paul was able to record them under the inspiration of the Spirit of God. We are glad he did!

Christians can be kind individually as well as corporately: "But to do good and to communicate forget not: for with such sacrifices God is well pleased" (Heb 13.16). We are to put away all malice and be kind and tenderhearted to one another. Furthermore we are to have a spirit of forgiveness and love, "forgiving one another, even as God for Christ's sake hath forgiven you ... and walk in love, as Christ also hath loved us, and hath given himself for us an offering and a sacrifice to God for a sweetsmelling savour" (Eph 4.32; 5.2). We are always eager to be forgiven but sometimes less willing to forgive.

The Sacrifice of our Praise
Wonderful opportunities and possibilities to honour God open up for us when we understand that every word we speak, as well as every action we perform can be for His glory. When we think of praising God, we should not limit priestly service or worship to a specific time or place.

Our prayer lives can be marked by praise and thankfulness at many different times, for example, in our private times alone before God; when we gather with our families in our homes; when we meet together each Lord's Day with our brothers and sisters in Christ to remember the Lord Jesus in the breaking of the bread and drinking of the cup: "By him therefore let us offer the sacrifice of praise to God continually, that is, the fruit of our lips giving thanks to his name" (Heb 13.15). We are described as a holy and royal priesthood who show forth "the praises of him who hath called you out of darkness into his marvellous light" (1 Pet 2.5, 9).

The Sacrifice of our Preaching
Faithful preachers of the gospel worship as they preach. Their

hearts are full of praise, and overflow in exalting the Name of Christ when they point sinners to Him, the only Saviour. As men preach in that spirit, "a sweet savour" of Christ ascends to God.

Paul put it like this: "Now thanks be unto God, which always causeth us to triumph in Christ, and maketh manifest the savour of his knowledge by us in every place. For we are unto God a sweet savour of Christ, in them that are saved, and in them that perish: To the one we are the savour of death unto death; and to the other the savour of life unto life" (2 Cor 2.14-16). The preaching of the gospel carries the savour of His Name heavenward and also carries it far and wide throughout the earth. Those who refuse the Saviour are condemned. Those who trust in Him are saved and receive the gift of eternal life.

The background to Paul's remarks in 2 Corinthians 2 was the triumphal return of a Roman general after a victorious military campaign in a distant land. The victory parade entering Rome would have included the local politicians and city officials with their seals of office, the musicians playing their trumpets and harps, the soldiers bearing the spoils of war and the prisoners shackled together in their chains. There were also the priests waving the censers of incense. The air would have been heavy with the smell of that incense. To the prisoners it was the dreaded smell of defeat, even death. To the army the same smell signified victory and life.

The Sacrifice of our Persons

The greatest sacrifice we can offer to God is ourselves: "I beseech you therefore, brethren, by the mercies of God, that ye present your bodies a living sacrifice, holy, acceptable unto God, which is your reasonable service…that ye may prove what is that good, and acceptable, and perfect, will of God" (Rom 12.1-2).

The paradox is that through giving, we also receive (Phil 4.17). When the Philippians gave to God and to Paul, fruit was credited to their account. But the generosity of the Macedonian Christians went deeper than their pockets and exceeded the expectations of those who received their gift: "This they did, not as we hoped, but first gave their own selves to the Lord, and unto us by the will of God" (2 Cor 8.5). We can imagine the encouragement Paul received from the wholehearted kindness of these saints, many of whom were materially poor and no strangers to affliction themselves. What brought even more joy to his heart was that they had given themselves unreservedly to the Lord.

When Paul and his friends went to Thessalonica to preach the gospel, they endeared themselves to the people there, living amongst them and showing them the love of Christ. The whole venture cost them more than a sermon or two: "So being affectionately desirous of you, we were willing to have imparted unto you, not the gospel of God only, but also our own souls, because ye were dear unto us" (1 Thes 2.8). These references show that our bodies, our selves and our souls should all be consecrated to the Lord.

We can also see something of the character of the Melchisedec priesthood in the lives of others who stepped into the breach to help their brethren and sisters who were passing through times of severe trial. Throughout the book of Acts we read of the prayers of the saints for one another. When Peter was in prison, the church prayed unceasingly (Acts 12.5). Also when the Christians in Judaea were in deep need because of famine, Paul undertook a journey to carry a gift to them from the churches of Macedonia and Achaia. He reminded the Roman Christians that they too had a responsibility to help meet the needs of others less fortunate than themselves (Acts 11.28-29; Rom 12.13; 15.26).

Paul was cheered by the help of others when he was in prison. Likewise, through his letters written from the prison cell, he sent out encouragement to friends like Timothy and Titus. The constant two-way flow of help and encouragement was what marked those early followers of Jesus Christ. The giver was blessed through the joy of giving and the recipient was blessed in receiving. God received the praise and the glory in it all.

Any glory we bring to God or help we bring to others will never compare with that which Christ brings. Any sacrifice we make will never equal His. And yet, we can draw upon the mercy and grace of our Great High Priest in our own lives. Then, in some small measure, we can pass blessing on to others. This is what we should try to do at every opportunity.

PERSONAL REMINDER
To become more like Christ, I must:
- be full of praise to God
- honour Him in all that I do
- live sacrificially.

CHAPTER 15

Our Advocate with the Father

The Lord Jesus Christ is our Advocate with the Father as described in the first Epistle of John (1 Jn 2.1). He helps us deal with the reality of sin in our own lives. Once again we discover that Christ is the answer to all of the difficulties and challenges we face in life.

The problem of our sin

Sin is a problem to us all. For us to deny this is to deceive ourselves and to contradict what God has said in His Word (1 Jn 1.8, 10). We are all vulnerable and there can be no room for complacency. The world, the flesh and the devil have not gone into retirement, and every one of us is frail and feeble at best. Those who are quick to denounce gross forms of sin in others are often guilty themselves of pride, envy or some other equally destructive attitude. A woman who was caught in the act of adultery was completely forgiven by the Lord Jesus (Jn 8.11). Her critics, the scribes and Pharisees, slunk away in shame when Jesus challenged them as to their own condition. There is no record of them being forgiven.

Even the great men of the Bible were not sinlessly perfect; they had weaknesses just like us. They often failed on their strongest points. Abraham was a great man of faith, but he went down to Egypt and got into trouble when he failed to trust in God (Gen 12.10-20). Moses was described as one of the meekest men upon the earth but one day, in a fit of rage, he slew an Egyptian (Ex 2.12). Samson was known for his strength and yet, under the influence of a scheming woman, he became as weak as water. David rose high as a great king and a man after God's own heart, but he came crashing down through lust (2 Sam 11.1-5). Solomon was so wise at the beginning of his reign but so foolish at the end, sinking into gross idolatry (1 Kgs 11.1-8). Peter was bold in his claims of loyalty to Christ, but he was suddenly overcome with fear when confronted by a servant girl who identified him as a follower of Christ (Mt 26.69-75). Barnabas was usually true to his name ('son of consolation') and a great encouragement to others, but on one notable occasion he lapsed and sorely disappointed his colleague, Paul (Gal 2.13).

In his first epistle, John made sharp contrasts to show that the children of God should now be different from what they once were: he spoke of light and darkness; obedience and disobedience; love and hate; belief and denial; righteousness and unrighteousness; life and death. We will never attain sinless perfection in this life, but we are not at liberty to continue in sin. We who have been born into the family of God should be seeking to live a life of increasing holiness.

The Scriptures teach that although sin is a reality in all of our lives from time to time, it is not a defining feature in the life of a child of God. One of the reasons why John wrote his epistles was so that believers should not sin. Those who continue in habitual sin call into question the reality of their profession of faith in Christ: "Whosoever abideth in him sinneth not: whosoever sinneth hath not seen him, neither known him" (I Jn 3.6); "He that committeth sin is of the devil" (3.8); "whosoever doeth not righteousness is not of God" (3.10); "We know that whosoever is born of God sinneth not" (5.18).

John raised the possibility rather than the inevitability of a Christian sinning: "If any man sin, we have an advocate with the Father, Jesus Christ the righteous" (1 Jn 2.1). All of us are conscious of defilement in our lives. We have said things and done things that we have regretted. And living in a world marked by evil, all of us have a daily struggle to keep our minds and hearts pure. The Word of God and the Spirit of God work together to make us conscious of defilement. When we realize that we have sinned, we need to be cleansed. Without that cleansing our fellowship with God remains broken; our joy and peace are affected, as is our power for service. We do not lose our salvation but we no longer enjoy it. Thank God, Christ is the answer to this dilemma.

Christ's answer for our sin
We need to take two looks, as it were, to appreciate the way in which Christ is able to help us. Firstly, we look back to what Christ did on the cross to save us from our sins. Then, we look up to see what He does for us now as our Advocate in restoring fellowship with God after we have sinned. Even though, in our terms, these past and present ministries of Christ are separated by thousands of years, it is the blood He shed upon the cross that is the key to our cleansing even now.

We were completely forgiven when we first trusted Him. Even though we were burdened with our guilt, He received us and cleansed us. He had taken our guilt upon Himself and suffered in our place. That initial moment of trusting Him brought a change that was like being washed all over (as in Jn 13.10); however, as we travel home to heaven we become defiled along the way and we need frequent daily cleansing. This corresponds to the washing of the feet which Jesus did and of which He spoke in the upper room (Jn 13.8). John teaches that the blood shed on the cross has an abiding value and power to go on cleansing us day by day (1 Jn 1.7).

What are we to do when we become conscious of sin? Again, two things are central. Firstly, we are to confess it. This confession takes place before God. The sin is exposed and called exactly what it is, with no room for any cover-up or excuses. King David's prayer of confession in Psalm 51 had the following key elements: he cast himself in repentance before God, looking to His love and mercy alone; he hid nothing and minimized nothing; he blamed no one else; he desired to be rid of sin; he acknowledged the pain of discipline; he realized the importance of the heart and spirit (the inner man); he sought restoration of joy, fellowship and usefulness.

Secondly, after confessing our sin we are to forsake it; this is the result of true repentance. Victory is not always immediate and sometimes a struggle persists. Old habits die hard, but these can be overcome through His strength, not our own. A humble walk with God and complete reliance upon Him are the foundation pillars of a victorious life that honours Him. When we realize that He is everything and we are nothing, our love for Him grows and our desire to please Him deepens. Disobedience is no longer an option. That is not to say we ever come to an end of weeding out undesirable things from our lives that make us so unlike Christ. One of the greatest dangers in the Christian life is to become self-satisfied with our spiritual condition; "I am what I am, and have no need to change now" would seem to be the attitude of some. May we all go on striving to reach higher ground. If we are truly prepared to leave behind what we now are, we can change and become what we should be – more like Christ.

When we confess our sins, God is "faithful and just to forgive us our sins, and to cleanse us from all unrighteousness" (1 Jn 1.9). He is faithful to His promise and yet just, in keeping with His divine holiness. Through the death of Christ on our behalf and the shedding of His blood, those sins have been accounted for. God's just standard is maintained.

We need Christ as our Advocate to bring us back to the Father. The use of the word "advocate" in the English Bible has led some to view Christ's work in a legal setting. They regard Him as our representative who pleads in our defence when we sin. Perhaps a better way of understanding His work as Advocate is to appreciate that the original word means one who is called to our side to assist us in a time of need. In John's Gospel, the Holy Spirit is called the Comforter (*paracletos*). This is the same word which is used in 1 John. When we sin, we fall, and the link of fellowship with God is broken. Figuratively speaking, Christ comes to our side, helps us up again and leads us back to the Father; He assists us in the restoration of communion. This is a family setting, not a courtroom drama.

Christ is the only One who is qualified to bring us back into close fellowship with God. He is righteous, untainted by sin. He was the only One who could satisfy God when, upon the cross, He offered Himself as a perfect sacrifice for the whole world (1 Jn 2.2). There is a sufficiency in the finished work of Christ for all to be saved, but it is only effective for them that believe (Rom 3.22). Those of us who have trusted in Him have the assurance that our sins have been forgiven.

It is wise for us all to keep short accounts with God. A tender conscience and a sensitivity to sin should cause us to lift our voices often to God in confession so as to maintain the joy of daily fellowship with Him.

Helping others
Christians have a responsibility to assist one another and encourage the development of a Christlike character. This also applies to dealing with sin and its consequences.

On a personal level, we can help one another. In Galatians chapter 6, Paul was dealing with the knotty problem of the restoration of a believer who had erred and had quickly found himself in spiritual trouble. The exact nature of the fault is not clear, but it was public enough to be observed by others and serious enough to require intervention. The erring saint needed help, but it was only a spiritual brother who could render the appropriate assistance. Paul put it like this, "Brethren, if a man be overtaken in a fault, ye which are spiritual, restore such an one in the spirit of meekness; considering thyself, lest thou also be tempted" (Gal 6.1).

Most of us would hesitate to call ourselves spiritual but we cannot avoid the conclusion that in the case described, someone had to take the responsibility to act. This action was not to be that of a meddling busybody, but to be that of a concerned and spiritually mature Christian who was well aware that similar tendencies could be found in his own heart (6.1). That is why generous measures of humility, meekness and godly fear were prerequisites for such a ministry (v 3). However weak the helper felt, he would seek to act in love: firmly but gently (v 2). We must add a note of caution: the road to restoration is always blocked when sin is denied, and confession and repentance are not forthcoming.

The word used for "restore" was known in classical Greek as a medical term for the setting of a broken bone or dislocated joint. The three related principles of treating fractures (reduction, immobilization and rehabilitation) have become established over many centuries and there are parallel lessons which relate to the spiritual realm. Bones are broken due to sudden injury. The fracture is painful and potentially damaging if left untended. How then should the treatment proceed?

Firstly, a broken bone is reduced by bringing it into line again. Usually the surgeon exerts gentle but sufficient pressure to move the bone back to its original shape. In so doing he is causing something similar to a reversal of the injury that brought about the damage in the first place.

When a person falls into sin there is a serious break in his or her relationship with God. The treatment is painful but necessary for restoration to be effected. It requires a going back to where things went wrong: true repentance does not gloss over the problem or the underlying cause. Abraham went back to where he first erred, and we must do the same (Gen 13.3). A godly friend will be wise in counselling and guiding in this direction. There is always the temptation to try to short-circuit this vital step by excusing the sin or by using a rebuke that is as half-hearted and as ineffective as that which Eli gave to his sons, Hophni and Phinehas (1 Sam 2.22-25). Had Eli been firmer, he might have spared the nation, his boys and himself much tragedy.

Having brought the bone into line, it remains unstable and easily disturbed. Healing will take many weeks and so to assist this, the second principle is carried out: the affected member is immobilized and supported. Today we use plaster casts but the early physicians had their own means of splinting and traction so as to prevent unnecessary movement and to maintain alignment. A balance is important: too little restraint and the fracture will not heal; too tight a cast, and the blood supply will be compromised.

Regarding the believer, this reminds us that there are times when activity is inappropriate. Instead, one must come aside to rest and to reflect, so as to allow sound healing from the inside out. How long this takes will require fine spiritual judgment; resuming activity too soon may only add insult to injury.

The extreme end of spiritual breakdown is illustrated by the perplexing situation at Corinth. A man in the church was living openly in sin and this was not being dealt with in discipline. To Paul's distress, the church members were glorying in their tolerance of the illicit relationship. Their testimony in Corinth was seriously compromised; even unbelievers would have been ashamed of such conduct. For the upholding of God's honour, for the maintenance of the testimony and for his own good, the offender had to be removed from the church and excluded altogether from the sphere of corporate testimony and ministry (1 Cor 5.13). They needed to purify themselves by excommunicating the offender.

The healing process for a broken bone is often a lengthy one. Reduction brings the bone into line and immobilisation allows it to heal, but the final aim is for restoration not only of appearance but also, more importantly, of function. Success is not measured merely by a broken limb looking right: it must work right. Exercises are begun, but these are carefully graded and start slowly. By resuming gradual activity in this way the total healing of the fracture is encouraged until strength and usefulness are regained. The corresponding lessons in spiritual things are plain.

By the time Paul wrote his second letter to Corinth, the church had taken the necessary public action; however, having been slow to discipline the man at the beginning, it seems that they were just as slow to forgive him and receive him back into the fellowship. The implication was that the man had truly repented, but was being shunned. He was in danger of being overwhelmed by their rejection and lack of love (2 Cor 2.7). This was not to imply that the restored brother should have been thrust back into public activity – as we have noted already, that would have been unwise – but the process towards normal integration into the local church was to move in a positive direction. They were to receive him again.

All of us can find encouragement in the examples of restoration found in the Scriptures: Abraham, David, Peter and Mark are just a few. There is always great joy in true repentance as portrayed by the father who welcomed back the prodigal son (Lk 15.20). In that story the father did not go seeking his son immediately after his departure. Sometimes, in human terms, love calls for us to wait patiently and prayerfully for erring ones to come to their senses. When that happens and they turn around to take the first steps back, we should be more than glad to run and meet them on the way.

Today there are many surgeons who are skilled in treating broken bones; however, it would seem that the greater skills of assisting spiritual restoration are much harder to find. The Lord Jesus Christ is always ready to help us back to the Father. May we seek to be like Him and be prepared to help others back, if and when they fall into sin. Heaven will be filled with broken souls who have been restored by His loving touch.

A PERSONAL REMINDER
To become more like Christ, I must:
- encourage others to resist and overcome sin
- assist restoration when an erring one repents
- be willing to forgive.

CHAPTER 16

Our Friend

The Lord Jesus Christ displayed a real and enduring love for His friends. He was willing to share with them His innermost thoughts and the divine purposes that had been communicated to Him by the Father: "Henceforth I call you not servants; for the servant knoweth not what his lord doeth: but I have called you friends; for all things that I have heard of my Father I have made known unto you." He also set a clear standard and told them what He expected of them in the circle of His friendship: "Ye are my friends, if ye do whatsoever I command you" (Jn 15.14-15). Obedience means a great deal to Him.

Christ demonstrated the features of true friendship by His actions and taught the same by His words. We shall consider some of these features and appraise our own responsibilities as we seek to follow His example.

Proving faithfulness

The twelve men that Christ chose to serve with Him soon learned that He would never leave them nor forsake them. He was available and loyal at all times. In the end, He would pay the ultimate price for them upon the cross and fulfil the truth of Scripture as none other had done: "Greater love hath no man than this, that a man lay down his life for his friends" (Jn 15.13). As His followers, the disciples were slow to learn and quick to make mistakes. Nevertheless, He continued patiently to teach them, even when they lacked the faith to trust Him fully. Sometimes His words fell upon deaf ears and seemed to have little effect upon their dull hearts. It was only after His resurrection that they would recall and understand much of what He had said.

They would prove how fickle they were when, in His hour of greatest need, they let Him down. In the Garden of Gethsemane, He looked for their support and comfort in the face of His agony, but they could not even keep awake. When Judas arrived with an armed mob to arrest Him and gave Him the treacherous kiss of betrayal, Christ addressed him with these words, "Friend, wherefore art thou come?" (Mt 26.50). Those words must have echoed in his heart until the day he took his own life. Later, the other disciples forsook Jesus and fled. Peter would deny Him three times. Had the disciples been our friends, we probably would have felt we had endured enough of their disloyalty, and written them off: not so the Lord Jesus. He would soon entrust eleven of these men with the furtherance of His kingdom upon earth.

Promoting growth
Spiritual growth comes through being nourished with the truth of God's Word and by living it out in a practical way each day. The Lord Jesus kept this necessary balance with the disciples. We find Him teaching them and then sending them out to serve Him in the world. Christ made sure His disciples were first taught and then tested in service.

The Master gave them the secret to growth and fruitfulness: it was to abide in Him (Jn 15.4). This meant enjoying daily fellowship with Him and following Him faithfully. When they did this, His power would flow through them. They would bear not just "fruit", but "more fruit" and "much fruit" (Jn 15.2, 5). He was the vine and they were the branches. We all know how quickly a cut flower begins to wither, when severed from the main plant. In the same way, if we neglect fellowship with Christ, our lives will soon become dry and barren. We do not lose our salvation but our testimony will suffer; it will not count for much in the eyes of others. The fruit of the Spirit will not be manifested in us as it should be.

In the book of Acts there are shining examples of men in touch with the Lord. When Peter and John visited the temple in Jerusalem, they brought blessing to a lame man by healing him. Then, Peter boldly proclaimed the gospel of a risen Christ to the many onlookers. His audience, though perhaps critical of being addressed by two unsophisticated Galilean peasants, could not deny one outstanding truth: those uneducated men "had been with Jesus" (Acts 4.13). It was true that they had known Jesus when He was upon earth, but even after His ascension, they were found walking in daily communion with their Lord; their lives were marked with the beauty and fragrance of Christ.

Confronting weakness
The Lord Jesus Christ had perfect knowledge of His disciples. Peter was often bold and brash, steamrolling his way through life. Jesus had to restrain him and even rebuke him at times. Too often he did not live up to his new name but acted like the old "Simon" (Lk 22.31; Mk 14.37; Jn 21.15-17). One minute, Peter could speak words that could only have been communicated to him from heaven itself: "Thou art the Christ, the Son of the living God." Christ gave his commendation, "Blessed art thou, Simon Bar-jona: for flesh and blood hath not revealed it unto thee, but my Father which is in heaven." The next minute, Peter could blurt out offensive words that the Lord had to censure immediately: "Get thee behind me, Satan: thou art an offence unto me: for thou savourest not the things that be of God, but those that be of men" (Mt 16.16-23).

One of the most difficult things to do is to seek to correct a friend. We need to tolerate a good many foibles in one another but occasionally there are issues that adversely affect someone's testimony. A good friend, after deep exercise and prayer, will point out these problem areas and, at the same time, give encouragement to overcome them. Others might prefer to shy away from confrontation and say to themselves, "Well, I have plenty of failings myself, so what right do I have to pick faults in my friends? I should just accept them as they are, or else I might upset them and bring our friendship to an end." This latter course is by far the easier one, but it may have a sad outcome when a friend's particular weakness, if left unchallenged, brings about a tragic fall.

Provoking excellence

A true friend will encourage others to rise higher. When Christ reminded His listeners of what the law said, He added a short phrase, "but I say unto you ..." (Mt 5.21-22); He gave His followers a much higher standard to aim for. He was looking for committed hearts that would seek to carry out the spirit as well as the letter of the law.

Under the Mosaic law, a person could respond to an insult by avenging himself in an appropriate way: "An eye for an eye, and a tooth for a tooth" (Mt 5.38). Jesus taught that one should be prepared to bear the same insult time and again. That was how He treated His own sufferings at the hands of men. To have had such almighty power at His disposal and yet to have allowed wicked men to abuse Him so disgracefully, verbally and physically, causes us to be amazed.

Christ also taught what has been called 'second mile religion': "And whosoever shall compel thee to go a mile, go with him twain" (Mt 5.41). In other words, when doing good, add extra. Do not limit your action to the basic minimum, but be prepared to exceed it. Do not be calculating, but be generous with your time and efforts in serving others.

These standards He set, so foreign to the world's thinking, put us to the test. We are all adept at self-preservation and quick to defend our own corner. Sometimes we are embarrassed by enthusiasm or excellence in others, when these show up our own deficiencies. And yet, by His grace, it is still possible to leave behind the plain of mediocrity and climb higher in the ways of Christ.

Challenging service
The Lord encouraged His disciples to have vision when He urged them to look at the great need of perishing souls and then be exercised to pray: "Lift up your eyes, and look on the fields; for they are white already to harvest" (Jn 4.35); "The harvest truly is plenteous, but the labourers are few; Pray ye therefore the Lord of the harvest, that he will send forth labourers into his harvest" (Mt 9.37-38).

Christ eventually commissioned these men to be the ones who would meet the need they had been praying about: "Go ye into all the world, and preach the gospel to every creature" (Mk 16.15). He would be intimately associated with them in every endeavour for His Name's sake. As a faithful friend, He promised them that He would be with them every step of the way: "Lo, I am with you alway, even unto the end of the world" (Mt 28.20).

Before He left them, Christ gave His disciples a further promise that was linked to a clear command: "But ye shall receive power, after that the Holy Ghost is come upon you: and ye shall be witnesses unto me both in Jerusalem, and in all Judaea, and in Samaria, and unto the uttermost part of the earth" (Acts 1.8). And so, a small band of men began a work, in the power of the Spirit of God, which would spread to every corner of the globe. Hazarding their lives for their Master, they turned the world upside down. When opposition came, they boldly confessed, "We cannot but speak the things which we have seen and heard" (Acts 4.20). They had become faithful witnesses who refused to keep silent.

Strengthening in trials
Life can be a stormy business at times. Several storms are

recorded in the Gospels when Jesus gave the necessary help and comfort that brought the disciples safely through. In the first storm, the trip across the Sea of Galilee was made at His command. As they journeyed, a great storm blew up and the ship filled with water so that there was imminent danger of the boat sinking. During the turmoil, Jesus was asleep. The disciples rushed to waken Him and, betraying their lack of understanding, they questioned His love and care for them: "Master, carest thou not that we perish?" (Mk 4.38). At that point, He did not correct them. Rather, He arose immediately and commanded the wind to cease. When calm was restored, He challenged their lack of faith.

In the second storm, again the disciples were obeying His command when they took to their boat. To walk a path of obedience in life does not preclude difficulties. On this occasion Jesus was absent, but praying on a nearby mountainside. When the storm arose they tried vainly to reach the shore. He saw them in their need and, in the darkest period of the night, He came to them, walking upon the water. That night, Peter did what no other man had done when he ventured out and began to walk upon the sea; however, when he took his eyes off the Master, he started to sink. Immediately Christ rescued him, and when they came into the boat, the storm ceased (Mt 14.22-33).

There were others that the Lord strengthened in their hour of need. When John the Baptist was languishing in prison, a personal word of reassurance from Christ was just what he needed: "Go your way, and tell John what things ye have seen and heard" (Lk 7.22). Christ never let any of His friends down, and we can still prove this today as we experience His constant, unfailing care.

Comforting in sorrow
Sickness and bereavement are two of the most devastating circumstances that we have to cope with. At such times, the

presence of a sympathetic friend is a great comfort. The Lord Jesus Christ was present at both bedsides and gravesides. He was able to bring healing, and in three instances, He restored life where death had occurred.

The story of the sickness and death of Lazarus portrays One who loved and cared. At first the news was brought, "Lord, behold, he whom thou lovest is sick" (Jn 11.3); then there was a restatement of that love: "Now Jesus loved Martha, and her sister, and Lazarus" (Jn 11.5). In His response to the crisis, we note how affectionately Christ referred to Lazarus: "Our friend Lazarus sleepeth; but I go, that I may awake him out of sleep" (Jn 11.11). At the graveside, He wept, and those tears made an indelible impression on the onlookers: "Behold how he loved him!" (Jn 11.36).

Many questions arise during a time of illness and bereavement. Jesus was aware of all of them, and knew the anxiety in the minds and hearts of the sisters. Their faith in Him was put to the test because of His apparent delay, but in the end glory was brought to God, joy flooded the hearts of Mary and Martha, and many believed on Him.

On being a friend

Men and women have always sought after friendship; however, in recent years, social networking has become popular with many people of all ages. Using computers, one can remain at home and make contact with others from around the world. 'Friends', as they are called (you do not even need to have met before), can be collected and added to one's list with a click of a mouse: some lists have hundreds of names. The whole process is so painless and convenient. But are all of these really friends?

Real friendship is costly. It seeks not only to give time to others but also to encourage them, so as to bring out the best in them. It may involve personal sacrifice, as we have seen. Taking time to visit a friend who is sick or passing through trials can sometimes mean much more than all the get-well cards and text messages put together: "A friend loveth at all times, and a brother is born for adversity" (Pro 17.17). Human physical contact brings a special comfort to us all. This was exemplified in the life of Christ and His apostles.

Paul was not a one-man band when it came to his service for the Lord. He had many friends and helpers to whom he paid generous tributes. When we read the last chapter of his letter to the Romans, we marvel at the variety of the names on his list. He had a detailed and personal acquaintance with all of these brothers and sisters in Christ. Some were married couples. Others were single women who had been a source of encouragement to Paul in his service. Without any hint of impropriety, he was fulsome and wholehearted in expressing his gratitude for their help. Some friends had opened their homes for Christian gatherings. Others risked their own safety and would have laid down their necks for him. He fondly mentioned those who were the fruit of his gospel labours. One can sense the deep feelings in the heart of Paul as he recalled those who had succoured him and bestowed much labour upon him. Even as he wrote, he appended the names of those who were associated with him prison. In his final letter to Timothy there is a touching reference to one called Onesiphorus (2 Tim 1.16-18). He had been unashamed to seek out Paul when he was imprisoned in Rome and visit him there. By so doing he had greatly refreshed the heart of the apostle.

Paul added a timely warning concerning those who would seek to divide the Christians. They were characterized by deceitfulness and selfishness, and they were to be avoided at all costs (Rom 16.17). Unity amongst friends and believers is precious to God and we all have our part to play in maintaining and promoting mutual love. Divisive teachings as well as gossip and rumour-mongering should be forthrightly rejected by each one of us, if we truly desire to be more like Christ.

James warned of another kind of friendship that could seriously harm any of us: "Know ye not that the friendship of the world is enmity with God? whosoever therefore will be a friend of the world is the enemy of God" (Jas 4.4). We should choose our friends carefully, and then work hard at keeping them.

A PERSONAL REMINDER
To become more like Christ, I must:
- be loyal to my friends
- encourage them in their faith
- support them in their trials.

CHAPTER 17

His Imminent Return For Us

Over two thousand years ago, Christ promised that He would come again for His own (Jn 14.3). Since then, Christians have proclaimed this truth to the world; and as they have lived in the expectation of His imminent return, their lives have been moulded by this hope. They have often been ridiculed for holding on to what some regard as an improbable belief. In Peter's day there were those who mocked and taunted, "Where is the promise of his coming? for since the fathers fell asleep, all things continue as they were from the beginning of the creation" (2 Pet 3.4).

From the earliest chapters of the Bible, there were promises made concerning a coming Saviour. Without going beyond the book of Genesis, we see Christ pictured and previewed in various ways: as the bruised seed of the woman (Gen 3.15); the substitutionary lamb that God provided (Gen 22.8); and the one cruelly rejected by His brethren and sold for a handful of silver (Gen 37.19-28). This 'scarlet line of redemption', as it has been described, can be traced right through the Old Testament.

Thousands of years later these same promises and pictures were fulfilled in Christ's first coming to earth to be the Saviour of the world. He was born in Bethlehem to a virgin called Mary. John the Baptist announced Him to be the Lamb of God who would bear away the sin of the world. Christ presented Himself to Israel as their Messiah but they rejected Him. Betrayed by Judas for thirty pieces of silver, He was taken away and nailed to a cross. There He shed His blood as the necessary price of redemption for a world of sinners and laid down His life for us; but before He died, He promised that He would return to His Father in heaven and then come back again for His own. Who would be so foolish as to think that the One who fulfilled those promises made so long ago concerning His first coming, would somehow renege in keeping His promise to come back again?

Christ explained in John's Gospel why He had to go away and leave His disciples. He told them, "In my Father's house are many mansions: if it were not so, I would have told you. I go to prepare a place for you. And if I go and prepare a place for you, I will come again, and receive you unto myself; that where I am, there ye may be also" (Jn 14.2-3). He was going back to heaven to prepare an eternal home for those who believed in Him. He would then come back and take them to be with Him for ever.

In the meantime, as He explained further, He would send His Holy Spirit to dwell in His people: "Nevertheless I tell you the truth; It is expedient for you that I go away: for if I go not away, the Comforter will not come unto you; but if I depart, I will send him unto you" (Jn 16.7); "And I will pray the Father, and he shall give you another Comforter, that he may abide with you for ever; Even the Spirit of truth; whom the world cannot receive, because it seeth him not, neither knoweth him: but ye know him; for he dwelleth with you, and shall be in you" (Jn 14.16-17). The indwelling Spirit of Christ would be with us for ever.

Peter explained why there seems to be a delay, at least in human terms: "The Lord is not slack concerning his promise, as some men count slackness; but is longsuffering to us-ward, not willing that any should perish, but that all should come to repentance" (2 Pet 3.9). This is a brief but powerful statement which testifies to God's love for lost sinners. He does not want any of them to perish; in His mercy He is holding back, to give them time to repent.

When will He come?
How much longer will God wait for sinners to repent? And when will Christ return? Not one of us knows.

It is true that there are many signs indicating we are living in "the last days", as the Scriptures call them. No one can ignore the rising tide of lawlessness and evil. We hear politicians promoting ambitious plans to tackle the deepening world crises – global warming, international terrorism, economic recession, and the AIDS epidemic, to name but a few. The various world bodies set up to tackle these problems (such as the United Nations, the World Bank, and the World Health Organisation) all look increasingly impotent, despite the rhetoric.

Students of prophecy have much to interest them too in the changing conditions in the Middle East. At the same time, caution is needed in interpreting recent history. The State of Israel has held on to that small tract of land bordering the Mediterranean Sea since declaring independence in 1948. When the Israelis defeated the Egyptians in the Six Day War of 1967, and took possession of the Sinai Peninsula, it seemed that this might be the outworking of the ancient covenant promise that God made to Abraham. The Lord had spoken of a large land for His earthly people, "from the river of Egypt unto the great river, the river Euphrates" (Gen 15.18). But in less than twenty years, all of the Sinai had been handed back! Events can twist and turn rapidly indeed, especially in the Middle East.

Clearly, the stage is being set for great events and days of tribulation to come, just before Christ returns to earth in glory and power. Notwithstanding these realities in the world today, not one condition needs to be fulfilled before Christ returns to the air for His Church. It is not at all delusional to believe that

His coming will be soon. We do not need to look for signs – we look for Him!

How will He come?

It will be sudden. The salient passages of Scripture on the matter indicate that every believer will be changed "in a moment, in the twinkling of an eye" (1 Cor 15.52). The Thessalonian believers were concerned that those who had already died in Christ might be disadvantaged when He returned. Paul explained to them that, on the contrary, these believers will be raised first with glorified bodies, fit for heaven. He described the order of the wonderful event in this way: "For the Lord himself shall descend from heaven with a shout, with the voice of the archangel, and with the trump of God: and the dead in Christ shall rise first: Then we which are alive and remain shall be caught up together with them in the clouds, to meet the Lord in the air: and so shall we ever be with the Lord" (1 Thes 4.16-17). Christ will not send a messenger or representative to act on His behalf – He will come back Himself for us! These truths are a great comfort to all of us who love Him, even as we wait expectantly for Him. The revelation of Scripture ends with the promise being reiterated three times that He will come quickly (Rev 22.7, 12, 20).

The venue for our reunion with Him will be *the air*, as we have read. By contrast, the Old Testament speaks of Christ's future return in glory to *the earth* – the Mount of Olives (Zec 14.4) – to deliver His people, Israel, and set up His visible kingdom down here. His coming to the air for the Church, His heavenly people, will precede His return to this earth. There is no hint in Scripture that the unbelieving of earth will hear the "shout", "the voice of the archangel" and "the trump of God", or even catch a glimpse of the departure of the redeemed. We recall that after the Lord Jesus Christ rose from the dead, the only people to see Him were His own followers. Many great things are experienced only by the faithful and concealed from those who do not believe.

One could speculate endlessly as to how this great event we refer to as 'the Rapture' will affect those left behind on earth. Millions of Christians will have disappeared leaving gaps in all levels of society. One of the most poignant tragedies will be that many families will suffer eternal separation, when the saved ones go and the unbelieving family members remain. Those who have heard the gospel and known the truth, but left the matter of their own salvation too late, will be tormented and full of despair. Other people might continue for a time with little obvious concern (some might even rejoice that the Christians have gone) until the seals are broken, the trumpets are sounded, and the bowls of divine judgment are poured out (Rev 6-18). Even then, despite these terrible events, mankind will not repent (Rev 9.20-21; 16.9, 11).

While we wait

If the truth of Christ's imminent return gripped us as it should, we would live in a completely different way. A Christian from a past generation was said to open the curtains of his bedroom every morning and looking heavenward say, "Maybe today, Lord." Then, in the evening, as he closed the curtains, he would gaze upwards again and say, "Maybe tonight, Lord." If Christ came today, we would surely want Him to find us waiting expectantly, longing for that moment of reunion.

This sure hope should govern our attitude to the things of earth. In fact, it will completely revolutionize our lives and liberate us. Many things that once seemed important will no longer have much significance or value. Fame and fortune will be of no consequence. Worries and anxieties about the future will disappear. We will hold on lightly to our possessions, knowing that one day soon we shall be letting them all go. We will avoid sinking roots too deep, remembering that we are strangers and pilgrims, and not here to stay. We will make plans carefully, investing much more in heaven than we do upon earth, in the assurance that heaven is our eternal home.

Our day-to-day living will change in other ways as well. Certainly, we would not want to risk becoming careless and being found either spiritually asleep or doing something sinful when He comes: "And now, little children, abide in him; that, when he shall appear, we may have confidence, and not be ashamed before him at his coming" (1 Jn 2.28). Holiness and godly fear mark those who hold this truth dear: "And every man that hath this hope in him purifieth himself, even as he is pure" (I Jn 3.3). It is obvious that sometimes our lives are grubby and indulgent because we have not yet felt the full weight of the promise of His imminent return.

If, on the one hand, we need to be prepared – He could come today – then, on the other hand, we need to be patient in waiting for the vindication and reward of our life's work and service. James wrote, "Be patient therefore, brethren, unto the coming of the Lord. Behold, the husbandman waiteth for the precious fruit of the earth, and hath long patience for it, until he receive the early and latter rain. Be ye also patient; stablish your hearts: for the coming of the Lord draweth nigh" (Jas 5.7-8). Peter encouraged the Christians of his day to remember that their suffering and trials were only "for a season" or "a while" (1 Pet 1.6; 5.10). The outcome of patiently enduring is eternal glory. It is a divine and unchanging principle that glory always follows suffering.

In view of His soon return, our service will be markedly different. We will keep in mind the shortness of the time that is left: "I must work the works of him that sent me, while it is day: the night cometh, when no man can work", said our Lord Jesus (Jn 9.4). He felt the need of the moment and focused on the task in hand, being aware that the time for working would soon be past. Our preaching will be invested with a passion that is so often lacking. We will beseech men and women to be reconciled to God while there is still time to do so. Sometimes this note of urgency is absent, and instead of preaching that "now is the accepted time" (2 Cor 6.2), we give the impression that it would be all right to think things over for a while and receive Christ next week, or even next month. In personal witnessing too, we should always be ready to give "a reason of the hope" that we have in Him (1 Pet 3.15).

The greatest motivation for service is love to Christ: this produces faithfulness and diligence as we work and wait for Him. We wait joyfully, for we have a living and a sure hope (Rom 12.12; 1 Pet 1.3; Heb 6.19). The early Christians gazed upwards as they watched the Lord leave them from the slopes of Olivet and ascend in the clouds. They were assured by two angels that "this same Jesus" would return in the same manner as they had seen Him go into heaven (Acts 1.11). Great comfort and reassurance are found in these words.

A little further on in the book of Acts, there was another man with an upward look. His name was Stephen and he was being stoned to death by a vicious mob because of his faith in Christ. He had lived for Christ, spoken for Christ, suffered for Christ and at the end, he was prepared to die for Christ. There is something even more precious – Stephen lived *like* Christ, spoke *like* Christ, suffered *like* Christ, and finally, died a violent and unjust death, just *like* Christ. As the stones rained down upon him, "he, being full of the Holy Ghost, looked up stedfastly into heaven, and saw the glory of God, and Jesus standing on the right hand of God, And said, Behold, I see the heavens opened, and the Son of man standing on the right hand of God" (Acts 7.55-56). Stephen was given a royal welcome home and His Lord, normally seated, was standing to receive him. Our Lord waits for us; are we waiting for Him?

There is a great welcome reserved for us too. Presently, many of us are accustomed to gather as the first Christians did on the first day of the week, to remember the Lord by breaking the bread and drinking the cup; by so doing, we are proclaiming His death "till he come" (1 Cor 11.26). When He returns for us and we see Him as He is, face to face, we will no longer need the symbols of remembrance.

What a blessing it would be if He was to come soon, and we were to go home to heaven without dying! Let this simple prayer be often upon our lips, reflecting the true desire of our hearts, "Even so, come, Lord Jesus" (Rev 22.20).

A PERSONAL REMINDER
To become more like Christ, I must:
- hold the things of earth lightly
- look daily for His coming
- long more earnestly to see Him as He is.

CHAPTER 18

Our Eternal Glory With Him –
Like Him at Last!

The future is assured for the child of God. After the journey of life down here is over, heaven will become our eternal home. But heaven would not be heaven without Him, our blessed Lord and Saviour.

Resembling Him
What will it be like when we see Him for the first time, face to face? How shall we feel? Many writers have stretched their minds and hearts to try and imagine that day. John, under the inspiration of the Spirit of God, wrote that "we shall see him as he is" (1 Jn 3.2). His radiant glory will be revealed to us. That moment will be the fulfilment of all our hopes, and, at the same time, only the beginning of our eternal joy in heaven.

Above and beyond the fact of seeing Him as He is, and being with Him for ever, is the wonderful truth that we shall also be like Him at last! The glories and beauties of Christ will actually shine from us. In that day our spiritual vision will be clear, our minds will be free, and our hearts will be pure. There will be no more struggles with sin and no more distractions of earth. Spiritual dullness will no longer restrict us and time will no longer constrain us. We will continue to learn more and more of the greatness and glory of our Lord; indeed, there will be no end to our ongoing education in the things of God.

Seeing Him as He is, we will then be able to love and praise Him as we ought. Words will come readily to our lips as we join the choir of heaven and sing in perfect harmony of His worthiness: "Thou art worthy ... for thou wast slain, and hast redeemed us to God by thy blood" (Rev 5.9). We will add our voices to that Hallelujah chorus: "Worthy is the Lamb that was slain to receive power, and riches, and wisdom, and strength, and honour, and glory, and blessing ... Blessing, and honour, and glory, and power, be unto him that sitteth upon the throne, and unto the Lamb for ever and ever" (Rev 5.12-13). Furthermore, we will serve Him and be joyfully busy there (Rev 22.3). No joy ever experienced upon earth can compare with the eternal bliss that awaits us.

Christ will share His glory with us. Peter described himself as "a witness of the sufferings of Christ, and also a partaker of the glory that shall be revealed" (1 Pet 5.1). He taught that even though we have been called to glory, the pathway to it is one of suffering: "But the God of all grace, who hath called us unto his eternal glory by Christ Jesus, after that ye have suffered a while, make you perfect, stablish, strengthen, settle you"; (1 Pet 5.10; 2 Pet 1.3). On the same theme, he included a fitting doxology in praise of His Lord: "To him be glory for ever and ever. Amen" (1 Pet 5.11).

These truths were enunciated also by Paul who suffered much for His Lord. He showed that we are joint-heirs with Christ and "if so be that we suffer with him ... we may be also glorified together." He continued, "For I reckon that the sufferings of this present time are not worthy to be compared with the glory which shall be revealed in us" (Rom 8.17-18). Throughout his life as a follower of Christ, Paul knew what it was to focus upon his Lord and to be gradually "changed into the same image from glory to glory" (2 Cor 3.18). That process would be perfected one day: "When Christ, who is our life, shall appear, then shall ye also appear with him in glory" (Col 3.4).

Rewarded by Him

Following our union with the Lord Jesus Christ in heaven, two important events will follow. The first will be the review of our individual lives and service at the Judgment Seat of Christ. All that we have done for Him will be assessed by His all-seeing eye. Secret things will be revealed and our motives will be laid bare; He will "make manifest the counsels of the hearts: and then shall every man have praise of God" (1 Cor 4.5). Self-serving deeds carried out in pride will go unrewarded, but humble acts of genuine love and devotion will not be forgotten by Him.

The quality of our service – likened to various building materials – will be tested by the fire of His penetrating gaze. Cheap and light materials that cost us little will be seen to be worthless and will burn up just like wood, hay and stubble. Investments that were weighty and costly in terms of personal sacrifice will be like gold, silver and precious stones (1 Cor 3.12). These will endure the fire and receive their commensurate reward. Christ's opinion will be the only one that matters and His commendation will be the only one that counts.

He will give crowns to those that have been faithful to Him. There will be a crown of righteousness for those who in love waited expectantly for His return (2 Tim 4.8). The incorruptible crown will be reserved for those who have sought and achieved victory over sin (1 Cor 9.25). A crown of life will be given to those who have patiently endured trials and opposition; some, like Stephen, were faithful even unto death (Jas 1.12; Rev 2.10). A crown of rejoicing will reward those who have been soul-winners (1 Thes 2.19), and a crown of glory will be a special honour conferred upon those who have diligently shepherded God's flock (1 Pet 5.2-4).

It is clear that a Christian can receive more than one crown. In a sense, that is all we shall have in heaven – the rewards of what we gave to Christ while down here upon earth. And what will we do with those crowns? Surely, we will do as the twenty-four elders did: we read that they fell down in worship before Him that sat on the throne and "cast their crowns before the throne, saying, Thou art worthy, O Lord, to receive glory and honour and power: for thou hast created all things, and for thy pleasure they are and were created" (Rev 4.10-11). We will give them all back to Him!

The second great event in heaven, the Marriage Supper of the Lamb, is described in Revelation 19. The bride, the Lamb's wife, is the Church, and each believer from this present age of grace is part of that Church. Her beauty is described in figurative language: "Let us be glad and rejoice, and give honour to him: for the marriage of the Lamb is come, and his wife hath made herself ready. And to her was granted that she should be arrayed in fine linen, clean and white: for the fine linen is the righteousness of saints" (Rev 19.7-8). The righteousness spoken of in these verses is really a plural word referring to those deeds that we have performed for the sake of our Lord. And so it is that the manner of our living down here can contribute to the beauty of that scene up there.

Reigning with Him
While we are enjoying the bliss of heaven above, the earth below will be convulsing and reeling from catastrophic events of unparalleled dimensions in a time of great tribulation. Millions will die in torment. The nation of Israel will be the focus of such severe hatred that it will seem close to annihilation. Even already Israel's enemies have boasted of their evil intention to wipe the nation off the face of the earth. When all seems bleak and the situation is at its most perilous, Christ will return.

He will come back to earth in manifest power and glory. His first coming to earth and to Bethlehem was almost unnoticed, except by a faithful few; however, when He returns as the triumphant King, He will take vengeance upon the godless and the unbelieving: "Every eye shall him, and they also which pierced him: and all kindreds of the earth shall wail because of him" (Rev 1.7). At the same time, He will be glorified in His saints (2 Thes 1.7-10). Having returned with Him, we will be associated with Him in the administration of His millennial kingdom, for "we shall reign with him" (2 Tim 2.12).

There are many more Scriptures in both the Old and New Testaments that point to this glorious millennial reign. But this period will only be a prelude to the eternal state of things when there will be "no more sea ... And God shall wipe away all tears from their eyes; and there shall be no more death, neither sorrow, nor crying, neither shall there be any more pain: for the former things are passed away" (Rev 21.1, 4). A new heaven, a new earth and the new Jerusalem will be inhabited by the Lord's own people from every age. In a special way the Church will permanently display to all the manifold wisdom of God (Eph 3.10). How sad to note that the unbelieving will have no part in this: they have nothing at all to look forward to, except the judgment of the Great White Throne, and eternal separation from God.

In 1 Corinthians 15.24-28 the scene of glory is described in this way, "Then cometh the end, when he shall have delivered up the kingdom to God, even the Father; when he shall have put down all rule and all authority and power. For he must reign, till he hath put all enemies under his feet. The last enemy that shall be destroyed is death...And when all things shall be subdued unto him, then shall the Son also himself be subject unto him that put all things under him, that God may be all in all." God will be satisfied in seeing His divine purposes fulfilled; Christ will be satisfied in seeing the great harvest that has resulted from the travail of His soul. We too shall be satisfied to be with Him and like Him for ever (Ps 17.15).

A personal note
The author has been privileged and blessed to have known a number of men and women whose lives were marked by a

radiant likeness to Christ. Not all were well known public figures. They would have been the first to admit that they were poor imitations of their Lord, and yet their personal acquaintance with Christ has left an indelible impression upon my life. Quite a number of them have already gone home to heaven and they are greatly missed, but the fragrance of Christ that marked their lives still lingers.

All of these different individuals were humble in character. At the same time, they were all supremely confident and joyful in Christ. They were all gentle in their demeanour, but underneath there was a strength that no one could deny. I remember them as being warm and accepting, but also wise and discerning. They were all kind and generous, seeking little for themselves; they dispensed encouragement and blessing whenever I met them. The love of Christ that filled them overflowed to me and to many others. Their lives made a mark for Christ and their example helped to mould my life.

Of course, it is a great mistake to be a slavish follower of men. Paul well knew this and so he exhorted others to "Be ye followers of me, even as I am also of Christ" (1 Cor 11.1). Paul was not interested in having an army of followers who would pledge their allegiance to him and duplicate his every action. Rather, he desired that they should imitate those features of Christ that were seen in his life.

He had laboured night and day in the gospel so that others would believe in the Saviour, and Christ would be *found in them* (1Thes 2.9). After their conversion, He had continued to labour and travail for his brothers and sisters in the faith, so that they might make progress in the things of God, and so that Christ would be more perfectly *formed in them* (Gal 4.19). Christlikeness was the supreme goal.

A closing wish (and prayer)
May we, the reader and author alike, make it our life's greatest

quest to become more and more like Christ, bringing glory to God and blessing to others.

May we walk in daily fellowship with God, guided by His Spirit and obedient to His Word, even as Christ lived, striving by His help to be faithful and true. May we be men and women of humility, simplicity, sincerity and tranquility. May we radiate warmth, joy, confidence and hope, even when trials and difficulties come.

May our love for the Lord be wholehearted and like His own love – impartial, sacrificial and unconditional. May it be freely expressed in our words and deeds, and overflow to our families, fellow-believers and those who have not yet believed in Him. May we be enabled to forsake love of self and of the world to realize this goal, remembering that we are citizens of a better land and we are on our way home.

May we consecrate our time, talents and treasures to Him, showing a Christlike care for others who might stray or struggle on the way. And each day, may there arise from our lives a sweet savour of worship and service that delights His heart. May we prove to be true and loyal friends who build and bind the people of God.

May we long to see Him and live in the light of His imminent return. And should we go home to heaven before that great event, may we leave behind us many lives that have been touched by Christ and transformed by His grace. When at last we see Him face to face and become perfectly like Him for ever, may we hear Him say, "Well done, good and faithful servant."

> *And is it so? I shall be like Thy Son!*
> *Is this the grace which He for me has won?*
> *Father of glory! Thought beyond all thought;*
> *In glory to His own blest likeness brought.*

Not I alone; Thy loved ones all, complete,
In glory round Thee there with joy shall meet!
All like Thee; for Thy glory like Thee, Lord!
Object supreme of all, by all adored!

J N Darby

Select Bibliography

Bellett, J. G. *The Moral Glory of the Lord Jesus Christ*; Bible Truth Publishers, Oak Park.

Crawford, N., et al. *The Person of Christ*; Gospel Tract Publications, Glasgow, 1987.

Darby, J. N. *Pilgrim Portions*; G. Morrish, London.

Edersheim, Alfred. *Jesus the Messiah*; Longmans, Green and Co., London, 1916.

Farrar, Frederic W. *The Life of Christ*; Cassell and Company, London, 1901.

Hewlett, H. C. *The Glories of our Lord*; John Ritchie Ltd, Kilmarnock, 2001.

Lucado, Max. *Just Like Jesus*; Word Publishing, Nashville, 1998.

MacDonald, William, et al. *God the Son*; Everday Publications, Toronto, 1974.

McConnell, Frank. *Christ the Lord*; Christian Publications, Cape Town, 1985.

Pentecost, J. Dwight. *Designed to be Like Him*; Discovery House, Grand Rapids, 1994.

Pentecost, J. Dwight. *The Words and Works of Jesus Christ*; Zondervan, Grand Rapids, 1981.

Rendall, Robert. *The Greatness and Glory of Christ*; Pickering and Inglis, London, 1956.

Stott, John. *The Incomparable Christ*; Inter-Varsity Press, London, 2001.

Walvoord, John F. *Jesus Christ our Lord*; Moody Press, Chicago, 1969.

Wilkins, Michael J. *In His Image*; Navpress, Colorado Springs, 1997.

Yancey, Philip. *The Jesus I Never Knew*; Zondervan, Grand Rapids, 1995.

Scripture Index

Life's Greatest Quest